NUMBER 115

# Yale French Studies

## New Spaces for French and Francophone Cinema

# Yale French Studies

James F. Austin, *Special editor for this issue*
Alyson Waters, *Managing editor*
*Editorial board:* Thomas Kavanagh (Chair),
 R. Howard Bloch, Edwin Duval, Tara Golba,
 Christopher L. Miller, Jean-Jacques Poucel,
 Julia Prest, Maurice Samuels, Yue Zhuo
*Editorial assistant:* T. Chapman Wing
*Editorial office:* 82-90 Wall Street, Room 308
*Mailing address:* P.O. Box 208251, New Haven,
 Connecticut 06520-8251
*Sales and subscription office:*
Yale University Press, P.O. Box 209040
New Haven, Connecticut 06520-9040
Published twice annually by Yale University Press

Designed by James J. Johnson and set in Trump
 Medieval Roman by The Composing Room of
 Michigan, Inc. Printed in the United States of
 America by the Vail-Ballou Press, Binghamton,
 N.Y.

ISSN 044-0078
ISBN for this issue 978-0-300-11822-3

JAMES F. AUSTIN

# Editor's Preface: New Spaces for French and Francophone Cinema

French Cinema is what Pierre Nora famously termed a *lieu de mé-moire*, a memory site, not only for the films that further a given cultural memory, but also for its institutions and places, whether the *Cahiers du cinéma* or Henri Langlois' *Cinémathèque*, recently moved from the Palais de Chaillot to its current site across the Seine river from the *Bibliothèque Nationale de France: François Mitterand*. Near the book-like, imposing structure built to protect France's near-sacred repository of written learning, civilization, and culture, we find then a similar *haut-lieu* of French prestige, its *Cinémathèque* and *Bibliothèque du film*, relocated, significantly and rather transnationally—surely gesturing to cinema's "always already" transnational status—in the former American Center, built by (North) American architect Frank Gehry. Perhaps most crucially, the space of France itself has taken on increasing importance in the cinema (echoing the number of articles in Nora's collection devoted to the geography of France),[1] whether in the many *banlieue* films, in the depiction of industrial cities in the north of France, or in the landscapes of the films of directors such as Bruno Dumont.

The last *Yale French Studies* volume on cinema—"Cinema/Sound" was published in 1980. Since then, French film has had many historical markers, particularly the centennial of cinema in 1996. In that time, film and visual studies scholars have built a prominent place for French cinema—not just in French departments but also in the humanities in general, where it has become a legitimate and valued field

---

1. *Les lieux de mémoire*, ed. Pierre Nora (Paris: Gallimard, 1984–1992); *Realms of memory: Rethinking the French Past*, ed. Pierre Nora and Lawrence D. Kritzman, trans. Arthur Goldhammer (New York: Columbia University Press, 1996–1998).

**YFS 115,** *New Spaces for French and Francophone Cinema,* ed. James F. Austin, © 2009 by Yale University.

of academic inquiry characterized by rapid growth and momentum. The cinema of the 1980s and first half of the 1990s has been thoroughly explored in such influential treatments and anthologies as those of Phil Powrie, Guy Austin, Susan Hayward, Ginette Vincendeau, and René Prédal.[2] This volume, then, focuses on the most current configurations of contemporary cinema, and particularly on the last ten to twelve years.

An art of space and time, the cinema invites reflection on both, and this has been especially true in a French context that has produced the theoretical treatments of Gilles Deleuze, who redefined the history of the cinema in terms of a transition from the (spatialized) movement-image to the time-image. Now, in 2009, at the fifty-year anniversary of the beginning of the New Wave, which proved essential to the evolution of French cinema, the question of what defines that cinema today is a particularly rewarding field of inquiry, all the more so that any stable category of a "French" national cinema itself loses meaning as France reconsiders what its own space consists of. The traditional idea of France has been increasingly unsettled by, for example, the civil unrest in France's suburbs in 2005, in which the spatial periphery of France's cities, long rejected from the body politic, staged a "return of the repressed." The continued working through of the memory of Algeria, and, more broadly, a reexamination of the relationship of France to its former colonies in the francophone world poses a similar question about where France begins and ends. One sign among many of the unresolved nature of France's expansion into African space during colonial rule, is the recent controversy around a 2005 law that proclaimed *le rôle positif de la présence française outre-mer* (the positive role of the overseas French presence); in the end, after after much outcry, the most offensive part of the law was repealed. France's ongoing relationship to the space of its territory within the Hexagon—to its cities and its multi-ethnic suburbs in which live many of those and the children of those who immigrated to France from the colonies—is properly political, engaging the *polis*, the city at the heart of the political, just as its relationship to its former overseas possessions in West and North

2. Phil Powrie, *French Cinema in the 1980s: Nostalgia and the Crisis of Masculinity* (Oxford: Clarendon Press, 1997); *French Cinema in the 1990s: Continuity and Difference*, ed. Phil Powrie (Oxford: Oxford University Press, 1999); Guy Austin, *Contemporary French Cinema: An Introduction* (Manchester: Manchester University Press, 1996); *French Film, Texts and Contexts*, ed. Susan Hayward and Ginette Vincendeau. (London: Routledge, 2000); René Prédal, *Le jeune cinéma français* (Paris: Nathan, 1998).

Africa raises the question of transnational political realities and configurations.

As Henri Lefebvre once suggested, each mode of production or each hegemonic force, whether political, economic, or otherwise, produces its own social space.[3] And indeed, reconfiguring space may be, in turn, one means to effect a fundamental economic and political change (Lefebvre, 408–412). Given its prestige, financial importance, and enormous cultural resonance in France, the cinema is well poised to engage in a spatial politics, to be an art of space producing its own space or spaces, and thus potentially redefining the space of France and the francophone world. In other words, at a time when the contemporary French and francophone cinema has reconstituted itself as a multiplicity of national, transnational, and postcolonial spaces, it is also asking the question of what is France, what is French space, how is space invested with meaning, and how can one contest those meanings. It is time, then, to look at what spaces—national, transnational, postcolonial, urban, suburban, and rural—"French" cinema has occupied and reconfigured.

The articles presented here explore how the filmic realm has been invested with spatial representations that in turn seek to reconfigure the French spaces of city, suburb, metropole, and (former) colony and the subjects that move through them: the *française* or *français*, the *blanc, black,* and *beur,* the immigrant and politician, and the (formerly) colonized. Thus we see the emergence of the "banlieue-film" such as *La haine* (*Hate*) (Kassovitz, 1995), with its spaces marked by otherness surrounding the urban centers, and the "immigrant film" such as *Inch'Allah dimanche* (Inch'Allah Sunday) (Benguigui, 2001), with its thematics of displacement: French cinema has begun to take into account a transnational space that encompasses not only (Paris-centered) metropolitan France, but also the "immigrant suburb" and the former colony.

A single work can never hope to answer all the questions raised here, but they have indeed informed the thinking behind this volume, which is divided into three sections: the first provides an overview of the cinema as it exists in France, in its current national and transnational configurations; the second considers the space of France in French cinema,

3. Henri Lefebvre, *The Production of Space*, trans. Donald Nicholson-Smith (Oxford: Blackwell, 1991). See especially chapters 1–2.

and notably examines that of the city, the suburb, and the countryside; the third section focuses on the francophone space of France's former colonies in Africa, and its exchanges with the space of the Hexagon.

Opening the volume, Michel Marie's article effectively grounds a discussion of French cinema in an understanding of what it has been historically since the New Wave. Marie lays out the successive generations of filmmakers that have followed the New Wave directors, the relationship of those generations both to the New Wave and to Bresson, and also to each other, while outlining the physical and economic situation of the cinema in France. If the funding mechanisms set in place over the past decades now favor the creation of first films by new directors, it is perhaps unsurprising to see a cinema open to new currents of filmmaking dealing with new realities and voices, those of women filmmakers, for example, or of transnational experience, or both as is the case with the vast array of women French/transnational directors discussed by Catherine Portuges in her essay here. These directors negotiate the borders of identity and community, those of France and other countries of appurtenance (for example North African nations), often doing so in France's multi-ethnic suburbs. A rich cinema with its own national or increasingly transnational dynamic prospers in France, then, but can this cinema be represented successfully when exported abroad? How the national French cinema changes as it represents itself in the international marketplace is the subject of Roger Celestin's piece, which argues that what is now exportable is a French cinema that represents French national space in stereotypical terms, making itself over as the image of easily understood "Frenchness," ready for consumption as such.

The question of how space is invested with meaning in the cinema, and to what such extent spatial engagements are political in nature is at the heart of the second section of this volume. Three spaces in this regard are critical—the city, the suburb, and the countryside. Margaret Flinn suggestively points to Chris Marker's de-centered politics that consist of occupying the city with painted cats in *Chats perchés* (Marker, 2004) (*The Case of the Grinning Cat*), cats that may be empty signifiers or, alternatively, herald, in an era of digital media "convergence," a new anonymous, collective, flash-mob style politics gesturing at new political formations arising in French urban space. After this discussion of a potentially new politics of the city, James Austin examines the struggle for political agency in the *banlieue,* and how cinema both diagnoses the problem and proposes a cure to the seemingly spatial problem of the suburb. That cinema about the *banlieue* predicted, for example, the violence there years before the 2005 riots, and now suggests as a solution the elimination and even destruction of suburban space itself in order to change the current spatial coordinates and thus the political dynamic of a seemingly hopeless situation. If political struggles new and old vie for the space of the *polis*, the traditional space of political contestation, and its suburban other, Ludovic Cortade examines current representations of the rural space that traditionally defined much of France; he demonstrates how the landscape of the countryside is used in the cinema to depoliticize, that is, to evacuate politics, especially those of the Left, all while reviving an older, near-mystical conception of the "monarchical" body and state.

The space of Africa and its relationship to that of France are the subject of the final section of this volume. Often, African and French space seem to merge through the African diaspora—indeed, it becomes difficult to know what constitutes an African film, since many of them are made by directors living in France, and are about the diasporic African communities in France, including the *san-papiers* (undocumented immigrants). Dominic Thomas's article looks at these questions, offering an in-depth discussion of how some of these films negotiate African/ European space. It includes a particularly helpful discussion of how colonial-era restrictions and postcolonial funding mechanisms determine which films could and can be made about Africa by Africans, whose "cultural nomadism" offers some possibility for working around these restrictions. Guy Austin, building on Benjamin Stora's work on the memory of Algeria, and on Cathy Caruth's treatment of trauma, analyses films that "return to the site of trauma," that is, Algeria, especially as some of them are now, unusually, filmed in Algeria itself. The occupations and control of space that was an integral part of colonial French strategy is now mirrored in the way meanings are expressed spatially in these films. Algeria is a memory site the meaning of which is still very much in contention, as Panivong Norindr indicates in his treatment of *Indigènes* (Bouchareb, 2006), as he details a situation that dates back to a colonialism that encouraged a spatial confusion among colonial subjects about which country is the *patrie* (fatherland), and thus about which country is worth fighting for, France or Algeria.

This volume would not have been possible without the collaboration of so many. I would like to extend personal thanks to Grace An, who was instrumental in the conception of this project, and who supported its coming to fruition in so many ways. I hope she will be pleased to see the results of the time she gave to this endeavor. My gratitude also goes to Alyson Waters, the Managing Editor of Yale French Studies, whose excellent suggestions and careful editing shaped, in no small measure, what follows. I would like to thank as well the contributors to this volume, for their articles, of course, and also for their graciousness and their unflagging efforts. Finally, I owe a debt to Ramla Bédoui, who has been essential in contributing support both analytical and moral in nature.

# I. French National/ Transnational Cinema: An Overview

MICHEL MARIE

# French Cinema in the New Century

## THE ECONOMIC SETTING

"Cultural Exception" is a French expression that was highly touted throughout the world in the 1990s. It first appeared in the public debate in 1993, during the negotiations of the Uruguay Round held as part of the GATT (General Agreement on Tariffs and Trade), the predecessor of the World Trade Organization (WTO). The expression signifies excluding works of cultural identity from free trade regulations, on the grounds that such works could not be reduced to the status of ordinary goods. This policy aimed at preserving the national legal systems for organizing and protecting the film, radio, and television industries confronted with the effects of the globalization of markets and the expected challenging of the Nation-States' competence and the privileging of vast, regional zones of free exchange.

The French film market is one of the only markets to escape the overpowering domination of Hollywood cinema and the dozen blockbusters it releases annually around the globe. Despite its relative success, the French market is nonetheless a threatened market, and is evolving in relation to the success of certain films that sustain and inspire, which are sometimes American and sometimes French. Until the beginning of the 1980s, French cinema held around 50% of its market. Subsequently, things stalled with a mean between 30% and 40%, and with a low point of 27% in 1986. Despite this relative decline, French cinema constitutes an exception in the world by its resistance to the Hollywood machine, often considered unstoppable. The French exception is due to a system of regulation that has become a reference for all countries aiming to find an economically viable alternative for producing and distributing film.

**YFS 115,** *New Spaces for French and Francophone Cinema,* ed. James F. Austin, © 2009 by Yale University.

The year 2000 was disappointing for French cinema because it held only 28.5% of the market. The following year, 2001, however, proved that French cinema was capable of recovery on its on own territory by relying on a certain diversity of production. It captured 41.5% of the market share, a level that it had not reached since 1986, thanks in part to popular comedies like *La vérité si je mens!2*[1] and *Le placard* as well as to genre films like *Le pacte des loups* and *Yamakasi*, and to *Le fabuleux destin d'Amélie Poulain*, a film that was an extraordinary success in France and in the world.

Occasionally, the blaze of publicity with which American blockbusters are released malfunctions. Thus, in 2002, despite its poster and its Oscars, *Chicago* didn't surpass 1.2 million tickets in France and was placed 36th at the box office, far behind Nicolas Philibert's *Être et avoir* (1.8 million tickets sold). Thus, a documentary film about a one-room classroom in a rural setting prevailed over a Hollywood super-production: an extraordinary example that proves that hierarchization isn't inevitably based on quantitative criteria or on excess if a certain diversity in film distribution remains intact. It is, in fact, the type of distribution that often determines a film's chances of finding its audience.

If we look at the years 2004 and 2005, the market shares for French films were around 36% to 38% for French film and 46% to 47% for American films. Obviously, the resistance of the national product remains fairly fragile and a new *Titanic* can easily overturn this delicate balance. The share of European films distributed in France varies between 8% and 15% of the total, which is very little, since this figure includes British films that are often in the Hollywood style.

The number of people in France going to the cinema has also withstood an inevitable decline. In the 1970s, there were, on average, 180 million spectators per year. The fleeting rise at the beginning of the 1980s preceded a brutal drop. Between 1982 and 1992, the number of tickets plummeted from 202 to 116 million. In the new century, attendance has started to pick up, reaching 175.5 million viewers in 2005 and 188.5 million in 2006. This rise is explained by two phenomena characteristic of the commercial reform of the past fifteen years: the modernization of the totality of theaters and the development of multiplexes on the one hand, and on the other, the creation of a "pass" allowing unlimited tickets for the equivalent of approximately $23 per month.

---

1. All titles of French films in this article are given in the original. For the translation of these titles, see the appendix at the end of the article. [Translator's note]

The first factor is the modernization of cinema theaters with a new commercial form, the multiplex, first created in the U.S., then imported to Belgium before coming to France. It is a system that adapts the market logic of retail business for the cinema. In 1993, Pathé opened the first French multiplex with 12 theaters and 2,650 seats. Five years later, there were 45 multiplexes in France. At the end of 2004, a dense network of 109 multiplexes took in 80% of all tickets sold. The multiplexes have effected a complete revolution in the commercial structure and are dominated by the chains UGC, Pathé, and Gaumont, and in Paris by MK2 as well. As a result, the independents have been marginalized. The massive expansion of multiplexes has completely changed the rules of distribution: a single film can be released on several hundred screens simultaneously on the same day, backed by a brief but intense marketing campaign on a national scale. This expansion also affects production. Market demand for films that one can target to a wide audience has largely prompted a return to genre cinema, privileging action films for young viewers, as in the *Taxi* series produced by Luc Besson and the light comedies such as those starring Gérard Jugnot, in the ever-popular series directed by Patrice Leconte (from *Les bronzés* in 1978 through *Bronzés amis pour la vie* in 2006). This demand for films with wider audience possibilities has also privileged the adaptation of light comedies from the theaters of the Paris boulevards like Francis Veber's *Le dîner des cons* (8 million viewers in 1998) and the remake of traditional films (Christophe Honoré's *Les choristes*, 8 million viewers in 2004). In each case, there is a more or less generic style and an obliteration of the concept of the *auteur*[2] or individual style. French cinema thus currently consists of the co-existence of a popular cinema based on genres, mainly comic, and an *auteur* cinema with a much smaller public. This phenomenon is confirmed by the extraordinary commercial success of Dany Boon's *Bienvenue chez les Ch'tis* (2008), a triumph of the "ethnic" comedy contrasting the south of France with the Pas de Calais in the north.

The second factor is the development of customer loyalty through the cinema "pass," first introduced by UGC in 2000 and followed by 3 other chains (Pathé, Gaumont, MK2). This further emphasized an economic division into two distinct sectors: big-budget films distributed

---

2. In the cinema, an *auteur* is a filmmaker with a personal style of filmmaking like a literary author. The concept is part of the legacy of the French New Wave. [Translator's note]

in several hundred copies and all the other films, distributed for a limited audience.

Finally, another transformation is both technical and economic. The appearance of the new digital technology has encouraged small budget films and has succeeded in completely upending the film production chain. The success of Agnès Varda's documentary essay *Les glaneurs et la glaneuse* (2000), illustrates this phenomenon that is developing above all in the field of the documentary film or essay, focusing on the private world of people's feelings and relationships. But the new digital technology also plays a part in big budget productions, as in *Vidocq*, with aesthetic results that are highly debatable.

The economic survival of cinema in the theaters has thus prompted a quantitative renewal in production. The number of films approved by the Centre National de la Cinématographie or CNC went from 141 films in 1995 to 212 in 2003. This approval concerns all films produced and co-produced by French cinema. If we confine ourselves to fully French films, the number rose from 97 films in 1995 to 183 films in 2003.

The year 2005 set a record of 240 films produced, of which 187 were French initiatives, 126 were completely French, 61 were co-productions, and 53 were mostly foreign. Obviously, this was a lot, and more than the theater market could absorb. Several dozen feature-length films were thus produced but received practically no distribution, and thus were not seen by the public. Clearly, there is a crisis of overproduction, and production in 2006 and 2007 only confirmed this tendency: 203 films in 2006 of which 164 were French initiatives; 228 films in 2007 of which 185 were French initiatives and 133 were completely French.

## FIRST FILMS AND FILMS BY WOMEN

Who makes these films? Here again, French cinema is distinguished by two elements: the large number of first or second films, and the number of female directors. The first phenomenon dates back to the 1970s. Since then, the number of first films has increased from year to year, and today accounts for 40% of the total number of films made. Let us look at just the past few years: in 2000, there were 53 first films; in 2001, also 53; in 2002, 67; in 2003, 68; in 2004, 54; and finally in 2005, 60. In 2005, these 69 first films represented 37% of the total of feature films undertaken by the French. To that number, we should add 34 second films. Thus, 103 films out of 187 French films produced in 2005 were either a director's first or second feature film. On the one hand, there is, undeniably, a clear stimulating effect that makes it easier to direct a film and that encourages new experiences and experiments, but that is in the long run unfavorable to the development of a real career for a filmmaker, beyond a second film.

All things considered, French cinema has thus been very open to young *auteurs* in the past thirty years. Between 1988 and 1997, 329 young filmmakers made their first feature, with an average of 33 first films per year. In the subsequent five years, from 1998 to 2002, there were 293 first feature films, or an average of 58 first films per year.

Between 1994 and 2003, 499 persons in France were approved as filmmakers. It is obvious that only a tenth of them, say about fifty of them, were able to achieve relative fame in France, and even more rarely, internationally. We find a list of them in René Prédal's *Le jeune cinéma français* (republished under the title *Le cinéma français des années 90* in 2002 and 2008). Such notoriety is all the more difficult to achieve because the previous generations of filmmakers are still producing new works every year.

A parallel evolution is at work with the progressive feminization of the filmmaking profession. French cinema in fact can boast of the first female director in the history of cinema: the legendary Alice Guy, who worked for Léon Gaumont. Then there was Germaine Dulac who also worked in the silent cinema, and Jacqueline Audry in the 1950s. Agnès Varda is the female exception of the French New Wave. The year 1986, when several female directors presented a feature in the section "Perspectives of French Cinema" at the Cannes Film Festival, marks a major turning point. That same year, the entering class at La FEMIS, the national film school, included an equal number of young women and young men. In the twenty years from 1986 to 2006, dozens of young women became filmmakers. The pioneers are Claire Simon, Laetitia Masson, Claire Denis, Noémie Lvovsky and Anne Fontaine. For the most part, they are graduates of La FEMIS, but others have gained entry to the profession by writing scripts, making a short film, or by initially working as an assistant director. We could also mention here Christine Carrière, Emmanuelle Cuau, Judith Cahen, Solveig Anspach, Dominique Cabrera, Marie Vermillard, Sandrine Veysset, Hélène Angel, and many others. The recent César awarded in February 2007 to Pascale Ferran's last film, an adaptation of *Lady Chatterley*, represents the capstone of this phenomenon. But it is above all Catherine Breillat's provocative filmography that has made an impression, with her screen-plays centered on often autobiographical narratives and very personal sexual confessions (from *Romance*, [1999] to *Une vieille maîtresse*, a very daring adaption of Barbey d'Aurevilly made in 2005 and selected for Cannes in 2007).

How can we characterize in greater detail this "new women's cinema"? As an example, let us take a closer look at *Romance*. With her seventh feature, Catherine Breillat gained notoriety because of the film's scandalous nature. It has a reputation as the first feature film of a pornographic nature directed by a woman and distributed in the traditional commercial network. Although anyone under age sixteen was not admitted, the film was not "X-rated," and its "pornography" is limited to a few anatomical close ups of male and female genitals, framed in a very clinical manner. The title is ironic, because the story has really nothing of a sentimental "romance." It is the cold analysis of the masochistic depression of a young woman, whose partner no longer desires her. The narrative recounts what is a true ordeal for the heroine, Marie (played by Caroline Ducey), who gives birth at the end of the film to a little boy, while the father, Paul, dies in a gas explosion arranged by the mother. The medical metaphor dominates the film's visual style, as is demonstrated by the sequence of a gynecological exam in which an impassive succession of students look at the heroine's most intimate parts, shown in the realistic aesthetic of the scientific documentary. The filmmaker pushes to the maximum the antagonism among desire, sexuality, and feelings of love in opting for a dramaturgy that is anything but lyrical, and that unfolds in a modern apartment that has the sterile whiteness of a hospital room. Marie's masochism is made explicit in the red apartment of the school director, when he (Robert, played by François Berléand) organizes the classical ritual of the tying up of Marie's tortured body. *Romance* is a feminist, violently anti-male recounting of the Passion of Mary.

Thus, Breillat's women's cinema, often considered as "pornographic" or scandalous, is in reality much more analytical, indeed colder, than we might think. Her films prove that women directors have brought another idea of sexuality to the cinema, a far cry from romantic and sentimental clichés. The film's title should be understood ironically—there is nothing romantic about *Romance*.

## 4,323 FILMS IN TWENTY-FIVE YEARS

It is obviously no easy task to define the prevailing tendencies amid an ocean of films and directors, that is 4,323 films in 25 years, between 1980 and 2005 (an average of 172 per year). We have emphasized the youth of those making films. This is, of course, a direct result of the efforts and ideas of the New Wave filmmakers in the late 1950s. At the time, the profession was dominated by sixty-year-olds like Claude Autant Lara and Jean Delannoy, and needed new blood. This policy clearly prevailed and developed in the course of the 1980s, which saw a proliferation of sources of film financing (new television stations; pay channels like Canal Plus with production obligations; the creation of SOFICA, the Societé pour le financement du cinema et de l'audiovisuel; tax credits; etc.). Today, French cinema is a young cinema, in the sense that it is principally made by *auteurs* making their first films between the ages of twenty and thirty. If the generation of filmmakers in their sixties barred the way when Truffaut and Chabrol were young, today young filmmakers make up 80% of those directing films.

French production is thus full of contrasts and presents three very different groups. There are twenty or so seventy- or eighty-year-olds who are continuing to make new films. There is a host of young filmmakers who have made a first and perhaps second film. And then there is the category of directors between the ages of 30 and 50, where the competition is the fiercest. In this sense, film production mirrors the structure of the French labor market. For the sake of clarification, we can use the generational criteria to define important groups by intersecting the filmmaker's age with the date of his or her first film. Of course it is possible to make a first film very young, like Gaël Morel, who directed his first feature, *À toute vitesse*, at the age of 24, or much later in life, as Manuel de Oliveira who achieved international fame after the age of fifty.

## VETERANS OF THE NEW WAVE

The filmmakers of the 1959 New Wave have become the old guard of today's cinema. Born between 1920 and 1930, they are today between 77 and 87 years old! Some of them, like François Truffaut in 1984 and Jacques Demy in 1990, died prematurely. But Eric Rohmer (b. 1920, the senior member of this group), Alain Resnais (b. 1922), Agnès Varda (b. 1928) and Jacques Rivette (b. 1928), Jean-Luc Godard (b. 1930) and Claude Chabrol (b. 1930) are still directing and offer their latest films to their faithful followers on a fairly regular basis. They are thus a "bunch of still active veterans," in the humorous expression of Jean-Pierre Jeancolas.[3] To this canonical list, we should add Chris Marker, a maverick whose deeply original oeuvre oscillates between documentary and fiction, producing unique film essays like *Sans soleil* (1983), *Level Five* (1997), and *Chats perchés* (2004).

As for Claude Chabrol, he is building, film by film, the most homogenous oeuvre of all. Relying most of the time on a detective framework, he masterfully directs a few privileged actors. Isabelle Huppert is brilliant in his political film denouncing corruption after the Elf scandal[4] (*L'ivresse du pouvoir*, 2006); she was equally brilliant in *Violette Nozière* (1978) and *La cérémonie* (1995). In his recent films, *Secret défense* (1997), *Histoire de Marie et Julien* (2003), and *Ne touchez pas la hache* (2007), Jacques Rivette deepens his investigations of theatricality and the fantastic. If Eric Rohmer pursues his love stories from the "Moral Tales" to the "Four Seasons," he carries out very bold experiments in the domain of the historical film with *L'Anglaise et le Duc* (2001), *Triple agent* (2004), and most recently *Les amours de d'Astrée et de Céladon* (2007).

Alain Resnais and Jean-Luc Godard remain the two great formal experimenters of this group. While Resnais now strives to reach a large public with exercises based on popular songs, vaudeville, light comedies from the theaters of the Paris boulevards, and a troupe of faithful actors (*On connaît la chanson* in 1997, *Pas sur la bouche* in 2003, and *Cœurs* in 2006, with Lambert Wilson and Sabine Azéma), Godard on the other hand has withdrawn into his Swiss ivory tower to sculpt objects made of sounds and images. His recent films are less narrative and play increasingly on the visual and the musical (*Éloge de l'amour* in 2001 and *Notre musique* in 2004).

Among the Old Guard, Agnès Varda holds pride of place for young filmmakers because she uses digital technologies in a completely different fashion from others of her generation and is developing an autobiographical thematic close to their preoccupations (*Les glaneurs et la glaneuse* in 2000, then in *Deux ans après* in 2002, up to her installa-

---

3. See Jean-Pierre Jeancolas, *Histoire du cinéma français* (Paris: Armand Colin, Collection "128," 2005).

4. This was a vast and complicated politico-financial scandal that came to light in 1994, following an inquiry on the financing of the Biderman textile company by the oil company Elf. [Translator's note]

tions at the Fondation Cartier in 2005 and 2006: *Les veuves de Noir-moutier* and *L'île et elle*). Her approach in these works very often intersects the paths of her friend Chris Marker.

This "sextet" of distinguished old-timers keeps watch in the background. Their career achievements weigh upon the new filmmakers, who seek deliberately to distance themselves from the past. This is also true for the greatest French filmmaker of the postwar period, Robert Bresson, whose last film, *L'argent*, made in 1983, remains a benchmark that is as dazzling as it is unsurpassable.

It is a completely different story for the next generation, dominated by the tutelary figures of Claude Sautet (born in 1924) and Maurice Pialat (born in 1935). Both are biographical contemporaries of the New Wave filmmakers, born like them between 1920 and 1930, but who undertook filmmaking a little later and without having first worked as film critics. In the autumn of 1995, they both released their last films, *Nelly et Monsieur Arnaud* and *Le Garçu*, respectively, whereas their careers really emerged in the 1970s, after the New Wave. Maurice Pialat's *Van Gogh* (1991) inaugurated the 1990s, and is an undisputed *chef d'oeuvre* from this period.

Sautet and Pialat illustrate two principal, antagonistic film forms: the first is based on the classicism of writing, the second on the violence of live filming. In this sense, their films from the 1970s and 1980s have had a profound influence on new filmmakers of the last decades: from Arnaud Desplechin and Laurent Cantet to Catherine Breillat and Bruno Dumont. While Claude Sautet's films were recognized by certain critics, in particular critics from the review *Positif* as well as by a fairly large public, his films were mostly underestimated by the "auteurist" current coming from the *Cahiers du cinéma*. On the other hand, Maurice Pialat's creative violence was often venerated by young filmmakers in the 1990s, such as Xavier Beauvois, as well as by specialized critics.

## THE GENERATION IN-BETWEEN

The next generation includes filmmakers like Alain Cavalier, Jean Eustache, Jacques Doillon, Philippe Garrel, André Téchiné, and Claude Miller and a few dozen others depending on one's critical tastes. The aesthetic spectrum of this generation is relatively large. Certain *auteurs* intensify the New Wave aesthetic, like Jean Eustache, with *La maman et la putain* for its autobiographical dimension and its minimalist aesthetic, and Philippe Garrel from his experimental period (*Marie pour mémoire* and *Le révélateur*, both from 1968) up until his more recent films where the narrative is more substantial and there is more dialogue, from *J'entends plus la guitare* (1991), to *Sauvage innocence* (2001), and *Les amants réguliers* (2005). In the last film, which is unusually long (175 minutes) and which was awarded the Silver Lion at the Venice Film Festival, Garrel remains faithful to the aesthetics of *Le révélateur*. He constructs an intimist panorama of a group of romantic adolescents haunted by revolutionary myths and the spirit of revolt using flattering twilight images in black and white over spoken words. He confronts the generation of the father, that of Maurice Garrel, with that of the son, Louis Garrel, who embodies the rebellious young poet of the film. In contrast, André Téchiné and Claude Miller are situated in the aesthetic heritage of Truffaldian classicism. Miller even directed one of Truffaut's screenplays that Truffaut was never able to make himself (*La petite voleuse*, 1988).

Although none of his films has had a wide audience, Jacques Doillon's filmography is extraordinarily homogeneous. His manner of filmmaking is always based on the aesthetic of direct cinema, with a handheld camera and actor improvisation. He is even an example of a prolific French filmmaker since he has succeeded in making more than 30 feature films since the 1970s. Nonetheless, he remains completely unknown outside of France, even though his filmography includes such fascinating films as *La drôlesse* (1978), *Le petit criminel* (1990), *Ponette* (1996) and *Raja* (2003). This lack of appreciation is due no doubt to the actors' performances, the use of direct sound, the nature of the dialogues, and a generalized principle based on improvisation. (Still, it's worth adding that these same ingredients did not prevent John Cassavetes from becoming an internationally recognized filmmaker.)

## A "YOUNG FRENCH CINEMA"?

According to the critics, 1989–90 marked the beginning of a new tendency for "Young French cinema." Its manifesto film was Eric Rochant's *Un monde sans pitié* (1989). The provocative casualness of the main character, played by Hyppolite Girardot, is an up-to-date version of Michel Poiccard in *À bout de souffle*. But Rochant's work here is rather traditional. A whole constellation of young filmmakers, screenwriters, actors who originally met at La FEMIS gravitated around Rochant. Their unquestionable leader was Arnaud Desplechin, the most talented and ambitious of the group that also included the actor-director Matthieu Amalric, Noémie Lvovsky, and Pascale Ferran. Over time, certain members of this group have asserted themselves as *auteurs*, like Desplechin with *Esther Kahn* (2000), *Rois et reine* (2004), and *Un conte de Noël* (2008), and Pascale Ferran with *Lady Chatterley* (2007), which was awarded—as previously mentioned—the César for best film in 2007.

Lady Chatterley offers a conflicting vision of sexuality. It is Pascale Ferran's third feature, after ten years of silence, following her *Petits arrangements avec les morts* and *L'âge de possible* from 1994 and 1995 respectively. Admittedly, the adaptation of D. H. Lawrence's novel, *Lady Chatterley et l'homme des bois*, fits into a long French tradition of "heritage" films,[5] a tradition brought up to date by Patricia Mazuy with her very original *Saint-Cyr* (2000) and Olivier Assays's more conventional *Les destinées sentimentales* (2000), based on Jacques Chardonne's long-forgotten novel.

Pascale Ferran's film is much more personal and may be compared to Catherine Breillat's *Romance*. Ferran's film fits into a descriptive and analytic tradition whose source is the work of Robert Bresson. The first half of *Lady Chatterley* is intentionally slow. The heroine mopes around the English countryside filmed in general shots and panoramic shots of the trees and the forest. We are an hour into the story before the heroine first encounters the man-of-the-woods. This contact will completely change the perception of the world and of the surrounding nature, as much for the character as for the viewers. Pascale Ferran builds her film on a thematic and visual opposition, confronting the vast artistocratic residence, a metaphor of a tomb, and the gamekeeper's hut, uncomfortable but very alive. The direction of the actors favors gestures and glances over dialogue, until the man-of-the-woods' final confession. In the film's last scene, he lucidly emphasizes the insurmountable gap of social class that separates the two lovers.

There is thus a young cinema that comes out of La FEMIS. There is

---

5. James Austin, in his forthcoming book *Proust, Pastiche, and the Postmodern, or, Why Style Matters*, defines the French "heritage" film as a genre that usually enjoys a healthy-sized budget, often features well-known French actors, and takes as its subject the history and, often, the literature of France. Ferran's film is an adaptation of D. H. Lawrence's novel, *John Thomas and Lady Jane* (1927), an alternate and less well-known version of his infamous *Lady Chatterley's Lover* (1928). The earlier version, *John Thomas and Lady Jane*, is published in French under the title *Lady Chatterley et l'homme des bois* [Lady Chatterley and the Man of the Woods]. [Translator's Note].

a young women's cinema. There is also the completely new appearance of filmmakers who are immigrants or children of immigrants, either Arab or African. The North Africans are first of all actors and characters in the new French cinema. In this group, the actor Roschdy Zem, originally from Morocco, stands out with his impressive filmography: we find him in the work of Laetitia Masson (*En avoir ou pas*, 1995), Michel Spinoza (*La parenthèse enchantée*, 2000), Pierre Jolivet (*Ma petite entreprise*, 1999). In *Indigènes* (directed by Rachid Bouchareb), Zem is the lead actor and shares billing with his three acolytes: Jamel Debbouze, Samy Naceri, and Sami Bouajila.

Major directors in this category are Karim Dridi, who made his debut with *Pigalle* in 1994; Malik Chibane (*Douce France*, 1995); Abdellatif Kechiche (*La faute à Voltaire*, 2001); and Yamina Benguigui (*Inch'Allah Dimanche*, 2001). It was no accident that Abdellatif Kechiche's *L'esquive* won a César for best film in 2005.

How can we sum up the originality of Kechiche's film in just a few lines? *L'esquive* takes place near buildings in a low-income housing project on the outskirts of Paris. Kechiche films endless discussions in which young adolescents of diverse ethnicities (but predominantly North African and aged 14 to 16) confront each other. The young actors respond with a remarkable spontaneity and the camera frames their verbal exchanges in the tradition of the best of direct cinema. The script brings together Lydia, who is rehearsing for class a scene from Marivaux's *Jeu de l'amour et du hasard* with the timid Krimo (the nickname for Abdelkrim) who attempts to play the role of Harlequin in order to get closer to the girl he loves. Filmed with a lightweight camera at the end of autumn, all the scenes take place around the buildings, in the municipal garden or on the terraces of a modest outdoor theater, and in the surrounding streets.

The text of Marivaux's play acts as a developer for bringing out the French spoken in the low-income Paris suburbs, articulated at top speed, with its phrasing and authentic accents that differentiate each of the characters. Kechiche succeeds remarkably in recording the young women's disputes over seduction and jealousy, their obsessive talk about rehearsing, and the confrontations founded on insults and verbal aggressions that are both violent and ritualistic. The scene that brings face to face one of Lydia's girlfriends and the young gang leader who comes to take her cell phone is one of the most intense in the film, as is the somewhat more conventional scene of the police check, one particularly humiliating for the young high school students. Ten years after Mathieu Kassovitz's *La haine* (1995), the young French cinema depicts the youths of the low-income housing projects with a much greater authenticity, distancing itself from the style of advertising clips and the flashiness of postmodernism. With his third and still more ambitious and personal film, *La graine et le mulet* (2007), Kechiche has continued his success.

The first decade of the new century is also characterized by a consideration of French colonial history. In addition to *Indigènes* (2006), which presents Muslim combatants in the French army in 1943–44, the Algerian War is tackled in a direct manner by the young *auteurs*. In 2007, Philippe Faucon directed *La trahison*, a depiction of the conflict of conscience experienced by young Muslims wearing the French uniform in 1958. The previous year, the Austrian filmmaker Michel Haneke, in *Caché*, drew on the Algerian War as experienced in Paris, and the film's flashbacks are motivated by the repression of the demonstrations of the Algerian FLN. A French production, *Caché* won the best director prize at Cannes in 2005.

The recent period is also distinguished by the box office success of two new categories: documentary films and animation films. In the past, in France as in the rest of the world, documentary feature films very rarely benefited from a theatrical release. For the most part, they have been broadcast on the small screen or by other means (cassettes and DVD). From time to time, a documentary film has had an unexpected success. In the last decade, this phenomenon has become more regular in France, as well as abroad. It is crowned by the extraordinary box-office success of Nicolas Philibert's *Être et avoir* (2002). Several dozen films appear in this vein, including Rithy Panh's terrifying documentary *S21, la machine de mort Khmère rouge* (2002).

In order to illustrate the richness of French documentary, we will mention two recent films: Nicolas Philibert's *Retour en Normandie* and Sandrine Bonnaire's *Elle s'appelle Sabine*. Both of them fall within a certain strand of the New Wave that during a film shoot aimed to capture the unexpected, the unpredictable within the real—what Noël Burch called *l'aléa* (the unpredictable) in his *Praxis du cinéma*.[6]

Philibert's *Retour en Normandie* (2006) wasn't as successful as *Être et avoir* but it is every bit as fascinating. The "return" (*retour*) is that— thirty years later—of the filmmaker, who had been a young assistant to René Allio on the shoot of the film *Moi, Pierre Rivière ayant égorgé*

---

6. Noël Burch, *Praxis du cinéma* (Paris: Gallimard, 1969).

*ma mère, ma sœur et mon frère.* Philibert had taken part in the pre-production and casting of Allio's film, traveling all over the Norman countryside in order to find among the Calvados farmers non-professional actors who would play the characters of the family of the young murderer, and Pierre Rivière himself. For his film, he met with all the characters and questioned them on the influences of the film on their present lives, thus following the approach of a "making of" in reverse. The film's highlight is the appearance of Claude Hébert (who played the role of Pierre Rivière; he was also the young boy in Jacques Doillon's *La drôlesse*) in the second half, an explicit manifestation of the "unpredictable" before the filming began.

*Elle s'appelle Sabine* (2007) is the first documentary by the actress Sandrine Bonnaire, who was discovered by Maurice Pialat in *À nos amours.* It is a moving testimony to a young woman, Sandrine's younger sister, who has become gradually autistic. It is even more a testimony to the ravages of psychiatric internment and medication. The success of the film's approach is due to the honesty of the filmmaker, who also films herself; it is also due to the previous existence of numerous archival images of Sabine's adolescence recorded by members of the family. The documentary very astutely uses documents from the past juxtaposed with images from the present, framed by digital cameras and with direct sound. As with Nicolas Philibert, though in a different manner, Sandrine Bonnaire's approach depends on the hand-held camera and direct sound, techniques that have become much more flexible thanks to digital technology. Her approach is also developed by a parallel between the co-existence of times, drawing on the recorded images of an idyllic childhood and adolescence, and those of a merciless present of psychosis. More than ever, the cinematic recording of the real juxtaposes one time period with another, as André Bazin long ago intuited in his famous essay on the mummy complex.[7]

Animation films have been greatly stimulated by the CNC's production aid. The French school of filmmaking has become famous for films like *Kirikou et la sorcière* (Michel Ocelot, 1998), *Les triplettes de Belleville* (Sylvain Chomet, 2003), and *La prophétie des grenouilles* (Jacques Rémy Girerd, 2003). These films propose a very personal graphic universe, influenced by the richness of the French school of comic art. Simultaneously, Goscinny and Uderzo's popular comic in-

7. André Bazin, "The Ontology of the Photographic Image," *What is Cinema?*, vol. 1, trans. Hugh Gray (Berkeley: University of Calif. Press, 1969).

spired adaptation using very famous actors: Alain Chabat's *Astérix et Obélix. Mission Cléopâtre* (2002).

## THE RETURN OF OLD FORMULAS AND THE REAPPROPRIATION OF NATIONAL HERITAGE

*Les choristes* was the unexpected success of the 2004 box-office. Christophe Barratier's first feature-length film is a remake of a 1946 French film, Jean Dréville's *La cage aux rossignols*. It falls within the movement of national heritage reappropriation already at work in 1993 with Jean-Marie Poiré's *Les visiteurs*, which was inspired in large part by a classic of comic cinema from the 1930s, Christian-Jaque's *François 1er* (1937). In 2007, Michel Hazanavicius proposed a parodic rereading of espionage films from the 1960s with *OSS 117, Le Caire nid d'espions* with the actor Jean Dujardin, who was first discovered in *Brice de Nice* (James Huth, 2005), in the leading role.

## A GAMBLE ON THE FUTURE: FOUR MAJOR FILMMAKERS

If we attempt a somewhat subjective aesthetic appraisal of the new French directors to have emerged in the last ten years and who should be remembered, we can suggest four names: Cédric Kahn, Laurent Cantet, Xavier Beauvois, and Bruno Dumont.

Bruno Dumont, born in 1958 in Bailleul in the North of France, began his career as a philosophy professor and a director of documentary films. His first feature-length fiction film was *La vie de Jésus* (1996), followed by *L'humanité* (1999), which won the Jury's Grand Prize at Cannes. In 2006, he released his third feature, *Flandres*, which also won the Jury's Grand Prize at Cannes.

The second of these films, *L'humanité*, asserts the originality of his filmic style. Dumont is very definitely one of the major filmmakers of contemporary French cinema. His narratives are often linear, yet very elliptical. He masterfully uses the natural surroundings of Bailleul and its countryside. His characters are played by non-professional actors who are physically unattractive, and thus embody the opposite of the dominant aesthetic of the well-proportioned bodies of commercial entertainment cinema. Their acting is minimalist. He frames in a very geometrical manner the vast, open spaces of the Pas de Calais region, the furrows of plowed fields, rural paths, as well as the streets of mining villages with their straight rows of red brick houses. The summer heat exacerbates the heavy atmosphere that makes bodies sweat and the young woman, Domino (played by Séverine Caneele), strip. The characters' terseness is matched by the silence of the sound-track that foregrounds the blowing of the wind, the panting breath of the characters, and some scattered noises reverberating in the atmosphere. Music, when present, is interior to the fictional space and is very loud but fragmentary. The "mugs" of these actors are larger than life and forever mark the spectator, something that was understood by the filmmaker David Cronenberg, who gave best actor and best actress awards to Emmanuel Schotté (who plays Pharaon De Winter) and Séverine Caneele at the Cannes Film Festival. *Flandres* is situated precisely in this formal continuity. Dumont is definitely the direct heir of the most somber and the most despairing Bresson, that of *L'argent*.

Laurent Cantet (born in 1961), a student at l'IDHEC,[8] directed shorts and made documentaries for television, including *Un été à Beyrouth*, about the civil war in Lebanon in 1990. He then made three major feature-length films: *Ressources humaines* (1999), *L'emploi du temps* (2001) and *Vers le Sud* (2006). In the first film, he presents a factory where the workers' conflict comes between a son, a company executive, and his father, a simple laborer who risks being laid off. *L'emploi du temps* is based on a news story, the Romand case: after being laid off for economic reasons, an executive turns to pathological and criminal mythomania.

Set in Port-au-Prince, Haiti, in the 1980s, under the dictatorship of Papa Doc, *Vers le Sud* paints a rather cruel portrait of two American female tourists, both in their 50s, short on love and sex, whose lives are shattered by the passion they both feel for a very young Haitian teenager.

Cédric Kahn (born in 1966) was an assistant editor to Yann Dedet on Maurice Pialat's film *Sous le soleil de Satan*. He first tried his hand at directing with *Bar des rails* (1993), followed by *L'ennui* (1998), *Roberto Succo* (2001), and in 2004, an adaptation of Georges Simenon's *Feux rouges* (2004), where he transformed the acting styles of Jean-Pierre Darroussin and Carole Bouquet, who is literally unrecognizable. In 2005 he filmed *L'avion*, a children's story adapted from a cartoon.

Xavier Beauvois (born in 1967, in Auchel, in the north of France) first directed *Nord* (1992), then *N'oublie pas que tu vas mourir* (1996)

8. L'IDHEC, the French national film school, was renamed La FEMIS in 1986. [Translator's note]

and *Le petit lieutenant* (2005). Each of these three films is character-ized, in its own way, by a very authentic social integration: a working-class family in *Nord*, a student who learns he is HIV positive in *N'ou-blie pas que tu vas mourir*, and a young police officer in *Le petit lieutenant*.

All four practice an uncompromising cinema in the dual legacy of Bresson and Pialat. They have learned the lessons of documentary cin-ema and social enquiry, shaped by a very rigorous style of filmmaking. Xavier Beauvois and Bruno Dumont are both from Northern France, an area that has been particularly hard hit by the recent economic crisis. In *Ressources humaines*, Laurent Cantet is interested in the industrial crisis in France where he films class conflicts and economic layoffs. Bruno Dumont selects the rural landscapes of the great plains of the north and uses non-professional actors with a language that is very marked by the region and its accent. Cédric Kahn's filmography is more eclectic but he also practices a toned-down directing style, based on long shots and a way of directing actors heavily influenced by the tra-dition of Bresson. His portrait of a psychopathic killer in *Roberto Succo* is of rare dramatic intensity, worthy of its model, *L'argent*.

This "cinematographic school" is very different from the move-ment represented by Arnaud Desplechin, whose work is marked by the milieu of intellectual and cultivated Parisians. Of course, this latter movement also has its major films, such as Desplechin's recent *Rois et reine* (2004), which was more biographical and introspective in its in-spiration, and which featured his regular accomplice, the actor Ma-thieu Amalric playing opposite, once again, Emmanuelle Devos. In September 2007, we meet up again with Mathieu Amalric in a brilliant adaptation of François Emmanuel's novel *La question humaine*, di-rected by Nicolas Klotz. The film extends the critique of the organiza-tion of work in a contemporary multinational to a reflection on the his-tory of Nazi totalitarianism and its policy of extermination.

A certain tendency of French *auteur* cinema is thus particularly sen-sitive to the most violent contradictions of the contemporary eco-nomic system, as is confirmed by the frequent choice of old, run-down industrial sites, such as the cities of the North and those of Eastern France. The filmmakers display a social awareness that became explicit in the recent "Manifeste des 13," promoted by Pascale Ferran.[9]

9. Pascale Ferran launched the idea for this manifesto in February 2007 when she re-ceived the lion's share of awards at that year's Césars. In her acceptance speech, she ex-

These films are possible thanks to a French system of production aid, described at the beginning of this article. They are eligible for the Jean Vigo prize, which is awarded to the best first films, and are frequently selected for the Cannes festival where they sometimes receive special distinctions (At Cannes, *L'humanité* was awarded the Jury's Grand Prize, and in 2008 Laurent Cantet's most recent film, *Entre les murs,* was awarded the Palme D'Or).

These films are rather austere and very far from entertainment cinema. They are removed from the advertising aesthetic that characterizes mainstream cinema. They frequently employ non-professional actors or little-known actors, rarely stars. In such cases, the performance is always very different from what we find in traditional cinema. The models of both Bresson and Pialat, although differing remarkably from each other, are ever present, as, for example, with Jalil Lespert in *Ressources humaines* and in *Le petit lieutenant,* Aurélien Recoing in *L'emploi du temps,* and Stefano Cassetti in *Roberto Succo.* This kind of filmmaking culminates with the non-professional actors Bruno Dumont uses in all his films, such as Emmanuel Schotté and Séverine Caneele in *L'humanité,* or Adelaïde Leroux and Samuel Boidin in *Flandres.*

This cinema's style often opts for a slow rhythm and shots of long duration, in the manner of the films of Abbas Kiarostami or Victor Erice. These films offer a radical alternative to Hollywood blockbusters with their hysterical editing. They clearly represent the wealth of contemporary French cinema, more than ever explicitly a cinema of *auteurs.*

All things considered, and to offer a few parting reflections, recent French cinema is characterized by an undeniable vitality in terms of production, bordering on over-production. But it offers categories that are increasingly compartmentalized. There are first of all around twenty films with big commercial budgets intended for a large popular

---

pressed her fears for the future of a segment of French cinema, called "du milieu," meaning *auteur* film. A group of twelve other persons, made up of filmmakers, distributors, producers, and exhibitors (the "Club des 13"), rallied behind her and published their conclusions: *Le milieu n'est plus un pont mais une faille* (Paris: Stock, 2008). Decrying an increasing bipolarization between commercial productions and *auteur* films, the report was nonetheless dismissed by Christine Albanel, the French Minister of Culture. As a result, the "Club des 13" has now over 150 supporters among French filmmaking professionals. See Elizabeth Bouvet, "7e art: La réforme du 'club des 13'" at http://www.rfi.fr/culturefr/articles/100/article_64901.asp [Translator's note]

audience and that sometimes exceed all expectations, as was the case with *Bienvenue chez les Ch'tis*. There is a certain reappearance of genre films, with comedies of manners, serious police films, or parodic, national, comic films. There are films by confirmed filmmakers through successive generations, from the veterans of the "Old Wave," to young *auteurs* with their first films. The discrepancy among all these films is only increasing, and it is very difficult for young, ambitious filmmakers to exceed the threshold of certain budgetary limits, thus condemning them to a certain "austerity" in their productions. More than ever, filmmakers must take "a vow of poverty," to use Jacques Rivette's words.

*Auteur* cinema, with its multiple faces, is integrating the documentary experience acquired in the making of short or commissioned feature films. It is becoming gradually "feminized" and multicultural, as is attested by the Césars awarded to Abdellatif Kechiche (*L'esquive, La graine et le mulet*) and Pascale Ferran (*Lady Chatterley*) for best film—increasingly a cinema of *auteurs* of both sexes, as well as a cinema finally integrating France's colonial past.

—Translated by Sally Shafto

## APPENDIX

Alphabetical list of all French films mentioned in the article with their English titles. English titles are taken from: www.imdb.com. Where no English title already exists, a literal translation of the French title is given, unitalicized. When the English title is the same as the French original, the title is listed only once.

*A bout de souffle* (*Breathless*). Jean-Luc Godard. 1960.
*L'âge des possibles* (The Age of Possibles). Pascale Ferran. 1995.
*Les amants réguliers* (*Regular Lovers*). Philippe Garrel. 2005.
*Les amours de d'Astrée et de Céladon* (*Romance of Astree and Celadon*). Eric Rohmer. 2007.
*L'Anglaise et le Duc* (*The Lady and the Duke*). Eric Rohmer. 2001.
*L'argent* (*Money*). Robert Bresson. 1983.
*Astérix et Obélix. Mission Cléopâtre* (*Asterix and Obelix Meet Cleopatra*). Alain Chabat. 2002.
*L'avion* (The Plane). Cédric Kahn. 2005.
*Bar des rails* (*Railway Bar*). Cédric Kahn. 1991.
*Bienvenue chez les Cht'is* (*Welcome to the Sticks*). Dany Boon. 2008.

*Brice de Nice* (*The Brice Man*). James Huth. 2005.

*Les bronzés* (*French Fried Vacation*). Patrice Leconte. 1978.

*Les bronzés 3: amis pour la vie* (*Friends Forever*). Patrice Leconte. 2006.

*Caché* (*Hidden*). Michael Haneke. 2005.

*La cage aux rossignols* (*A Cage of Nightingales*). Jean Dréville. 1945.

*La cérémonie* (*A Judgement in Stone*). Claude Chabrol. 1995.

*Chats perchés* (*The Case of the Grinning Cat*). Chris Marker. 2004.

*Les choristes* (*Chorists*). Christophe Barratier. 2004.

*Un conte de Noël* (*A Christmas Tale*). Arnaud Desplechin. 2008.

*De battre mon cœur s'est arrêté* (*The Beat That My Heart Skipped*). Jacques Audiard. 2005.

*Les destinées sentimentales* (*Sentimental Destinies*). Olivier Assayas. 2000.

*Le dîner des cons* (*The Dinner Game*). Francis Veber. 1998.

*Douce France* (Sweet France). Malik Chibane. 1995.

*La drôlesse* (*The Hussy*). Jacques Doillon. 1979.

*Elle s'appelle Sabine* (*Her Name is Sabine*). Sandrine Bonnaire. 2008.

*Éloge de l'amour* (*In Praise of Love*). Jean-Luc Godard. 2001.

*L'emploi du temps* (*Time Out*). Laurent Cantet. 2001.

*En avoir (ou pas)/To Have (Or Not)*. Laetitia Masson. 1995.

*L'ennui* (Boredom). Cédric Kahn. 1998.

*Entre les murs* (*The Class*). Laurent Cantet. 2008.

*L'esquive* (*Games of Love and Chance*). Abdellatif Kechiche. 2003.

*Esther Kahn*. Arnaud Desplechin. 2000.

*Un été à Beyrouth* (A Summer in Beirut). Laurent Cantet. 1990.

*Être et avoir* (*To Be and To Have*). Nicolas Philibert. 2002.

*Le fabuleux destin d'Amélie Poulain* (*The Fabulous Destiny of Amélie Poulain*). Jean-Pierre Jeunet. 2001.

*La faute á Voltaire* (*Blame it on Voltaire*). Abdellatif Kechiche. 2000.

*Feux rouges* (*Red Lights*). Cédric Kahn. 2004.

*Flandres* (*Flanders*). Bruno Dumont. 2006.

*François 1er* (*Francis the First*). Christian-Jaque. 1937.

*Le garçu*. Maurice Pialat. 1995.

*Les glaneurs et la glaneuse* (*The Gleaners and I*). Agnès Varda. 2000.

*Les glaneurs et la glaneuse . . . Deux ans après* (*The Gleaners and I: Two Years Later*). Agnès Varda. 2002.

*La graine et le mulet* (*Couscous*). Abdellatif Kechiche. 2007.

*La haine* (*Hate*). Mathieu Kassovitz. 1995.

*Histoire de Marie et Julien* (*The Story of Marie and Julien*). Jacques Rivette. 2003.

*L'humanité* (*Humanity*). Bruno Dumont. 1999.

*L'île et elle* (The Island and She). Agnés Varda. 2006.

*Inch'Allah Dimanche* (*Inch'Allah Sunday*). Yamina Benguigui. 2001.

*Indigènes* (*Days of Glory*). Rachid Bouchareb. 2006.

*L'ivresse du pouvoir* (*A Comedy of Power*). Claude Chabrol. 2006.

*J'entends plus la guitare* (*I Don't Hear the Guitar Anymore*). Philippe Garrel. 1991.

*Kirikou et la sorcière* (*Kirikou and the Sorceress*). Michel Ocelet. 1998.

*Lady Chatterley*. Pascale Ferran. 2006.

*Level Five*. Chris Marker. 1997.

*La maman et la putain* (*The Mother and the Whore*). Jean Eustache. 1973.

*Marie pour mémoire* (*Marie for Memory*). Philippe Garrel. 1968.

*Moi, Pierre Rivière ayant égorgé ma mère, ma sœur et mon frère* (I, Pierre Rivière, having cut the throats of my mother, my sister, and my brother). René Allio. 1976.

*Un monde sans pitié* (*Love Without Pity*). Eric Rochant. 1989.

*Nelly et Monsieur Arnaud* (*Nelly and Mr. Arnaud*). Claude Sautet. 1995.

*Ne touchez pas la hache* (*The Duchess of Langeais*). Jacques Rivette. 2007.

*N'oublie pas que tu vas mourir* (*Don't Forget You're Going to Die*). Xavier Beauvois. 1995.

*Nord* (*North*). Xavier Beauvois. 1991.

*Notre Musique* (*Our Music*). Jean-Luc Godard. 2004.

*On connaît la chanson* (*Same Old Song*). Alain Resnais. 1997.

*OSS 117: Le Caire nid d'espions* (*OSS 117: Cairo, Nest of Spies*). Michel Hazanavicius. 2006.

*Le pacte des loups* (*Brotherhood of the Wolf*). Christophe Gans. 2001.

*La parenthèse enchantée* (*Enchanted Interlude*). Michel Spinosa. 2000.

*Pas sur la bouche* (*Not on the Lips*). Alain Resnais. 2003.

*Le petit criminel* (*The Little Gangster*). Jacques Doillon. 1990.

*Le petit lieutenant* (*The Young Lieutenant*). Xavier Beauvois. 2005.

*Ma petite enterprise* (*My Little Business*). Pierre Jolivet. 1999.

*La petite voleuse* (*The Little Thief*). Claude Miller, 1988.

*Petits arrangements avec les morts* (*Coming to Terms with the Dead*). Pascale Ferran. 1994.

*Pigalle*. Karim Dridi. 1994.

*Le placard* (*The Closet*). Francis Veber. 2001.

*Ponette*. Jacques Doillon. 1996.

*La prophétie des grenouilles* (*Raining Cats and Frogs*). Jacques-Remy Girerd. 2003.

*La question humaine* (*Heartbeat Detector*). Nicolas Klotz. 2007.

*Raja*. Jacques Doillon. 2003.

*Ressources humaines* (*Human Resources*). Laurent Cantet. 1999.

*Retour en Normandie* (*Back to Normandy*). Nicolas Philibert. 2007.

*Le révélateur*. Philippe Garrel. 1968.

*Roberto Succo*. Cédric Kahn. 2001.

*Rois et reine* (*Kings and Queen*). Arnaud Desplechin. 2004.

*Romance*. Catherine Breillat. 1999.

*S21, la machine de mort Khmère rouge* (*S21: The Khmer Rouge Death Machine*). Rithy Panh. 2003.

*Saint-Cyr* (*The King's Daughters*). Patricia Mazuy. 2000.

*Sans soleil* (*Sunless*). Chris Marker. 1983.

*Sauvage innocence* (*Wild Innocence*). Philippe Garrel. 2001.

*Secret defense* (*Secret Defense*). Jacques Rivette. 1998.

*Sous le soleil de satan* (*Under's Satan's Sun*). Maurice Pialat. 1987.

*Taxi.* Gérard Pirès. 1998.

*Triple agent.* Eric Rohmer. 2004.

*A toute vitesse* (*Full Speed*). Gaël Morel. 1996.

*La trahison* (*The Betrayal*). Philippe Faucon. 2005.

*Les triplettes de Belleville* (*The Triplets of Belleville*). Sylvain Chomet. 2003.

*Van Gogh.* Maurice Pialat. 1991.

*La vérité si je mens ! 2* (*Would I Lie to You? 2*). Thomas Gilou. 2001.

*Vers le sud* (*Heading South*). Laurent Cantet. 2005.

*Les veuves de Noirmoutier* (The widows of Noirmoutier). Agnès Varda. 2005.

*La vie de Jésus* (*The Life of Jesus*). Bruno Dumont. 1997.

*Une vieille maîtresse* (*The Last Mistress*). Catherine Breillat. 2007.

*Les visiteurs* (*The Visitors*). Jean-Marie Poiré. 1993.

*Vidocq* (*Dark Portals: The Chronicles of Vidocq*). Pitof. 2001.

*Violette Nozière.* Claude Chabrol. 1978.

*Yamakasi—Les samouraïs des temps modernes* (Yamakasi—Modern Samurai). Ariel Zeitoun and Julien Seri. 2001.

ROGER CELESTIN

# Lost in Globalized Space? A Certain French Cinema Abroad

> Maurice Chevalier waiving his boater, or Edith Piaf—the Little
> Sparrow—alone on a dark stage, holding a note interminably
> while one or two melodies are dashed off on the accordion. These
> overexposed portraits are from a set of lingering 1950's clichés,
> most of them hovering under a striped café awning: the silly beret,
> the comical moustache, a toy poodle or two and intellectuals seated
> around outdoor tables bantering with women in low-cut dresses
> whose cleavages must be ogled with condescending concupiscence.
> Dispersed around the landscape is the perennial trio of perky French
> protuberances: the cigarette, the baguette and that frail filigreed
> phallus of an Eiffel Tower.
>> —Marcelle Clements, "Sighing, a French Sound Endures"
>> *New York Times*, October 18, 1998

> You Americans are idiots. The proof of that is you admire Lafayette
> and Maurice Chevalier whereas they are, precisely, the biggest idiots
> of all the French.
>> —Jean-Paul Belmondo as Michel Poiccard in Jean-Luc Godard's
>> *Breathless* (1959)

This essay asks: how is it that French films that dominated world
screens, including American screens for so long (on the eve of World
War I, 70% of the films playing on international screens were French
productions; in 1907 "40% of total films receipts from the U.S. went to
French films")[1]—now manage to break the threshold of major commercial success on these markets only when they either re-present
some of the most stereotypical images of "Frenchness" or when they
conform to the norms of what is commonly referred to as "Hollywood
cinema"? There have been exceptions, such as Claude Lelouch's *Un*

---

1. Victoria de Grazia, *Irresistible Empire. America's Advance Through Twentieth-
Century Europe* (Cambridge, Mass.: Belknap Press of Harvard University Press, 2005).
Today the tables have been almost symmetrically turned; American films occupied 45%
of the French market in 2007, while French films took 43.7% of the market and films
from elsewhere 11.3% (Centre national du cinéma).

YFS 115, *New Spaces for French and Francophone Cinema*, ed. James F. Austin,
© 2009 by Yale University.

*homme et une femme* (*A Man and a Woman*, 1966), Edouard Molinaro's *La cage aux folles* (*The Bird Cage*, 1978), or, more recently, Luc Jacquet's *La marche de l'empereur* (*The March of the Penguins*, 2005). All these films were major international box office hits without belonging to one or the other of these categories, though *Un homme et une femme* may conform to a certain association of "France" with "romance," and, once the voiceover and music were replaced in the English-language version of *La marche de l'empereur*, there was precious little, if anything, to be identified as specifically "French" in this film. On the whole, exceptions have been few and far between and the overwhelming majority of French films that have broken through that threshold of international commercial success have either perpetuated a series of "mythical" images of "France" or have "gone Hollywood." In what follows, we will only address the first strategy, leaving aside what might be called the "Besson option," that is, the adoption by French cinema of genres, styles, and commercial practices traditionally associated with Hollywood. In the process, we will retrace the origins of the present situation, going back to that time when French cinema, rather than conforming to either of these options, often pioneered the way for all others.

Since this essay is written on the year of the 40th anniversary of "May 68"—with its millions of striking workers, flaming barricades, university students throwing paving stones at charging riot police in the streets of Paris, accompanied by Jean Luc Godard, camera in hand, walking and filming in those streets during that month of May, one of the decidedly iconic moments of postwar French life—it is fitting that this piece, devoted to the way in which figures of "Frenchness" play a role in French cinema on the international marketplace, begin with an allusion to one of the most visible figures of that turbulent time, Daniel Cohn-Bendit, aka "Danny the Red," former sociology student and student leader, and today a member of the European Parliament. A few years ago, at the time of the debate around the European common currency, Cohn-Bendit gave a talk at Columbia University about the "United States of Europe" in which he highlighted what he called the "cheese issue" in the following terms: those opponents of the euro who bemoan the drowning of national identities in a European sea or the disappearance of national tastes and traditions in a bland European no man's land are wrong. Take the small French (or Greek, German, Irish, or Italian, for that matter) cheese producer: he can continue to make his cheese on a small scale using traditional methods, as he did before, and sell his cheese exclusively on his national marketplace, as he did before; but in order to have access to the European marketplace, and reap the resulting commercial benefits, he must conform to the food safety regulations of that larger marketplace. A "win-win" situation, it would seem: no one loses (the traditional cheese makers can continue to make cheese, those who appreciate their products can continue to consume them), and everyone wins (those producers who conform to the international norms have access to a much larger market for their product). However, in his enthusiasm for and support of a Europe in which the grandchildren of people who had been killing each other a half century before would now be "buying their ice creams with the same euro," Cohn-Bendit was not fully taking into account the ways in which "international norms" in a globalized space reflect the very unequal mechanisms of the marketplace, and ultimately determine national and international consumer tastes. Would not, in the specific case of the "cheese issue," reserving exclusive access to the European marketplace for cheeses that conform to its food safety norms ultimately result in the gradual disappearance of the "small cheese" on both the national and European marketplace through the sheer proliferation and ultimate dominance on all markets of the standardized "big cheeses" (so to speak)?

A link between the "cheese issue" and the international film market is provided by a comment made by Jack Valenti, for many years the representative of the US Motion Picture industry, to the French delegate during the GATT (General Agreement on Tariffs and Trade) negotiations in the early 1990s. France was claiming a "cultural exception" for certain "products," most conspicuously in the audio-visual field:

> Jack Valenti: You make wonderful cheeses. Keep it up and let us, alone, make films.
> French delegate: You already make 95% of the movies. What more do you want
> JV: 100%, of course.[2]

In this exchange, we can find echoes of something that, referring to exoticism, Roland Barthes called "a sort of intellectual equilibrium based on recognized places,"[3] but inadvertently transposed here by Valenti to the economic realm of the division of labor, specialized tasks, and com-

2. http://understandfrance.org/France/FrenchMovies.html [consulted June 15, 2008]
3. Roland Barthes, *Mythologies,* trans. Annette Lavers (New York: Hill and Wang, 1984), 152.

parative advantages as applied to the making of movies perceived as "just another product." However, one must take into account the fact that films are *not* just another product in the French context. My parallel between cheese and film is not a mere rhetorical ploy but is indicative of a peculiarly French phenomenon reflected in the nation's very tax structure. The TVA (value added tax) is a mere 5.5% on cinema *as it is on food,* while it is 19.6% on just about everything else, reflecting the predominant place occupied by food and "culture"—in this instance cinema—in the nation's self-image.

That having been said, what would be France's "recognized place"? Is it, as Valenti, and as a certain Manichean vision would have it: the USA/Hollywood as the maker of "popular" and thus commercially successful movies that gather mass audiences, and France/Paris as a locus of "art films" or "small films" that cannot be very successful commercially, in particular in the international marketplace? Valenti's version of the domination of the "big cheese" in this domain is unequivocal: "We dominate world screens not because of armies, bayonets, or nuclear bombs, but because what we are exhibiting on foreign screens is what the people of those countries want to see" (de Grazia, 282). That Hollywood routinely practices a form of market dumping—selling its films at under their real cost outside the US, these films having made much or all of their money back already in the domestic market—and enjoys a much wider domestic market as well as an international Anglophone market predisposed to English-language films—are apparently not factors deemed worthy of mention by Valenti in his sweeping statement.

A single example taken from France's own time of dominance, from the invention of cinema to the eve of World War I, reveals that far from being a "natural" or fatal distribution of "recognized places," the situation described by Valenti is firmly rooted in historical circumstances and that France, too, was (and is) a "functioning mass society."[4] In the wake of Lumière and Méliès's pioneering trajectory, Louis Feuillade's adaptation of Marcel Allain and Pierre Souvestre's popular feuilleton, *Fantômas* is a case in point. The serial was released by the French company Gaumont, one of the powerhouses of the film industry at the time, in five episodes between May 1913 and April 1914. Daniel Gercke's comment on the connection between the commercial objectives of this

4. Lucy Mazdon, *Encore Hollywood: Remaking French Cinema* (London: British Film Institute, 2000), 4.

decidedly "popular" project and the paradigm shift that was occurring is worth quoting at length:

> Fantômas was made, not for the handful of slumming surrealists who would later canonize the early Gaumont serials, but to seduce the general public for the lowest cost per meter of film. The serial was devised to addict the public to the phantasmagoric commodity, and Fantômas becomes a habit for a Paris in the twilight as capital of the nineteenth century, on the eve of the rhythmed shocks of industrial Taylorism, the War to End All Wars, and the rise of technological mass media. More than any avant-garde provocation, Fantômas reveals to the paying public that life is getting fast, disjoint, profane, and polymorphous—it is the spectacle of the crowd priming itself for the distractions of the twentieth century.[5]

These "distractions" of the twentieth century are what Jack Valenti, among others, would simply call "entertainment." Yet, while France was, in this instance, the country to release the wildly successful Fantômas, the producer of this particular "commodity," it was also, in that beginning of the twentieth century, on the verge of losing its predominance in the domain of film production and distribution to a rising Hollywood while Paris was receding "in the twilight as capital of the nineteenth century"—emblematized by its Eiffel Tower, to which we shall return.

Is France's decline as powerhouse of international cinema to be then symmetrically attributed to a corresponding decline in geopolitical power at a particular historical juncture—Gaumont's predominance lost in the trenches of the War to End All Wars? To a certain extent, yes; but, here again, beyond any monolithic or Spenglerian interpretation of the shift in power from France-Paris to USA-Hollywood, the causes of this changing of the guard are to be located in a network of economic, political, and social factors superbly analyzed by Victoria de Grazia in her *Irresistible Empire: America's Advance Through Twentieth-Century Europe*, to which I am much indebted for the following summary of that pivotal period, one that saw the rise of Hollywood and the appearance of American films as international commodity. De Grazia explores the "myriad connections" ranging from massive investments and certain "sharp marketing practices" such as block booking (forc-

---

5. Daniel Gercke, "On the Eve of Distraction: Gaumont's *Fantômas*, 1913–14," *Sites: The Journal of 20th-Century/Contemporary French Studies. Popular Culture* 1.1 (Spring 1997): 157–69.

ing distributors to rent blocks of film rather than only the ones they wanted), selective licensing, product branding (via a star system), the concerted efforts of politicians and businessmen, and the vertical organization of the film business (gathering production, distribution, and exhibition), all of which enhanced "the industry's capacity to create a transnational taste culture much in the way it had created an all-American movie culture" (de Grazia, 300). The passage from "all-American" to "transnational" is a crucial one and is particularly indicative of the strategies at work. At first, movie audiences practiced a "nonchalant ecumenism," indifferently going en masse to see movies from a variety of national provenances. The fact that films were silent at that time facilitated the phenomenon. During the period of French dominance, the U.S. market, for example, "the world's fastest growing and most competitive, voraciously consumed releases of any provenance" (de Grazia, 294). However, a crucial development put a end to this undifferentiated consumption of movies: the American film industry's "precocious cultural chauvinism," which variously took the shape of selective licensing agreements and the denouncing of French-made "westerns" (initially, an exclusively Hollywoodian product that had been instrumental in branding films as "American") as "inauthentic": "The Indians gave it away: any red-blooded American could distinguish a genuine 'redskin,' meaning a befeathered, well-muscled white stunt man in brownface playing at ambushing settlers on sets in the southern California desert, from a fake, meaning a flaccid pony-riding horseman galloping around locations in the Camargues" (de Grazia, 297). The "precocious chauvinism" evident in this denouncing of "French cowboy movies" is symbolic of the passage from "all-American" to "transnational." In this instance, the French reaction was an attempt to appropriate their own national signs, already modernist emblems on their way to becoming stereotypes of nineteenth century culture, through a strategy of "copyrighting their patrimony" by "preventing foreign (meaning U.S.) film companies from exploiting as set backgrounds familiar national monuments like the Arc de Triomphe, the Opéra, and Notre Dame" (de Grazia, 307). Topping the list would, of course, be that "filigreed phallus" of French modernity, the Eiffel Tower. The attempt to "patent" structures as public as these proved to be fraught with legal and practical difficulties. Where the French authorities could sometimes prevent American companies from using them as backdrops, or at least make it logistically difficult, by refusing filming permission on specific occasions and for specific reasons (obstructing traffic, for example), the legal basis for preventing the use of these icons of France's patrimony in American films in general could not be established. As a result the "copyrighting" of French national monuments remained an essentially symbolic stance.

The trade wars and the debates over "cultural exception" or "cultural imperialism" of the 1980s and beyond were thus already well on their way early in the century. France's European bourgeois culture and peculiarly Jacobinist centralizing and universalist Republic would be the loser in that encounter, facing as it did the polymorphous originator of Fordism with its own claim to universalism, but of another sort. The year 1926 is symbolic of this opposition: while considerable funds from the American Congress were used to create a special Motion Picture Section whose mission was to promote the film industry as a business, the French government was granting to cinema the same legal rights enjoyed by the theater, "which in effect meant to declare motion pictures an art" (de Grazia, 307). This basic opposition between commerce and art, between bourgeois "high culture" and mass entertainment, which had already characterized the "old Europe"/U.S.A. divide, thus manifested itself again, this time in what was quickly becoming the major "cultural product" of the twentieth century: the movies. France's attempt to "copyright" the most emblematic signs of its modernist culture was symbolic in that regard: to standardization and its proliferation, it opposed the most ostensible signs of its venerable patrimony (Notre Dame, for example) as well as those more recent signs of its centrality in the advent of modernity (the Eiffel Tower, most ostensibly). The result of this ultimately uneven struggle between what had been and what was becoming, was the emergence of Hollywood after World War I as the uncontested leader in the movie business and the appearance of a new type of film that was already the harbinger of today's "international" blockbuster. Well before these later twentieth-century products, post-World War I American cinema was buoyed up as "continuity-editing devices established guidelines for constructing the narrative, [and] innovative camerawork and artificial lighting gave films a polished veneer unknown in the prewar period." In sum, de Grazia writes, "coming out of World War I, the Hollywood studio system was to the standardized, mass-produced, internationally marketed cultural commodity what Fordism was to the global consumer durable trade" (de Grazia, 298).

France had thus been without a doubt one of the inventors and popularizers of cinema in a chronological arc that ranges from Lumière and

Méliès up to the Gaumont distribution of *Fantômas*, to refer to only the example used in this essay. However, even if it continued to have a thriving national cinema after that time and up to the present day—indeed with India, Japan, and South Korea, France is one of the very few countries in which the national film industry holds its own in spite of American imports—on the international marketplace, by the end of World War I its cinema had to a great extent been replaced by Hollywood's "internationally marketed cultural commodity." This commodity variously took the shape of the early westerns France had sought to emulate, Charlie Chaplin's Little Tramp and his antics, up to the big blockbusters inaugurated by the incessantly *sequeled* products that became not just films but "franchises": *Jaws* (1975), followed by *Star Wars* (1977), *Rambo* (1982), *Superman, Batman,* and *Spiderman* (1978, 1989, 2002, respectively), to the most recent in this veritable gallery of comic book adaptations, *Ironman* (2008), all of which embodied that new, easily globalized recipe of *spectacularity:* rapid editing, action-driven narrative, a hyper-reality filled with special effects and color-infused images, but, dramatically and ideologically, a black and white world where "good" always triumphs over "evil," leading to the satisfying "oomph" of definitive closure, to be trumped only by the profit-driven return of a similar scenario via the sequel, often by way of a new evil to be faced by the "good guy." The early westerns that hit French screens during World War I, with their black hats versus white hats, which had been instrumental in "particularizing" American cinema in a more innocent age of "ecumenical" movie going, have come a long way indeed.

By the time Private Ryan landed on the beaches of Normandy in 1944, the commercial supremacy of the American film industry had been well established and Hollywood was ready to release (or to unleash, depending on one's point of view) the considerable number of films it had stockpiled during the war. A scene from Spielberg's *Saving Private Ryan* (1998) is in fact symbolic of the way in which certain figures of Frenchness functioned both in the postwar era and in the decades that followed. The group of GIs led by Tom Hanks' Captain Miller finds a moment of respite in the town of Ramelle—in reality, Saint-Lô—now a mass of rubble after the allied bombings. After the violence of the beach landings and the encounters with German snipers, there is a lull, a brief moment of quiet as the soldiers sit around and, out of nowhere, a voice rises above the rubble, Edith Piaf's, the Little Sparrow's, at the time already a famous star, an emblem of France, singing one of those mournful hymns to unrequited love (*Tu es partout*, followed by *C'était une histoire d'amour*). One of the soldiers translates for the others as they all partake of that quintessentially French genre, the *chanson*. In that moment, even as the height of her career is still in the future, Piaf is *already* to those soldiers the sign of a formerly dominant culture that survives through its most emblematic, even stereotypical figures. As for the audiences of the late 1990s, as well as for today's audiences, whether French or international, Piaf, burnished by the intervening decades, has joined the gallery of clichés that have come nostalgically to represent France. The gum-chewing, cigar-chomping American GIs are also emblems and clichés of a culture. However, the U.S. *continues* to produce and disseminate its cultural clichés— from California surfers and black leather jacket-donning rebels, to trench-coated private eyes and sequined rock stars—in the globalized space it has been instrumental in creating, just as France had been central in the advent of a modernity symbolized by the "Haussmanized" spaces of Paris and other French cities in the nineteenth century. As Jean Baudrillard has proposed, although globalization, that twentieth-century development, is not exclusively or specifically "American," the United States was and remains a "strong pole" of globalization,[6] a position resulting not only from its geopolitical power, but from, among other factors, its ability to disseminate its practices and its culture; more specifically and accurately, it is the peculiarly popular appeal of American culture in an age of mass culture that facilitates the dissemination of the figures it produces in an era of American geopolitical domination.

France itself has continued to thrive as a culture and as a nation, but the world it was instrumental in creating, a world in which it was also a major political and cultural power, has changed. As a result, the figures of "Frenchness" that have potency—that is, box office clout—beyond its borders today are those that belong to that former time of dominance, of *rayonnement*, a time when "culture" was either modern bourgeois culture, or "popular culture," but in the French sense of *culture populaire*, with its echoes of "folk" or *terroir*-connected culture (rather than the English-language sense of "mass culture"). In the French gallery, we find figures ranging from the baguette-carrying,

6. Jean Baudrillard, "Jean Baudrillard: Interview with Roger Celestin," trans. Alyson Waters, *Sites: The Journal of 20th-Century/Contemporary French Studies. Popular Culture* 1.1 (Spring 1997): 5–15.

beret wearing, village-dwelling peasant of Provence, Louis XIV-the "Sun King," Marie-Antoinette, and Napoleon, to the starving artist in his Parisian garret, the "French lover," and the velvet-snooted Parisian minx. It is thus no accident that these are the figures that retain potency for audiences watching the French films that do break the threshold of international commercial success in a time of mass culture. These figures are *recognizably* "French," having already gone around the world in a former time of dominance and then later consumed as "French," bearing as they do the marks of that national provenance.

Before French cinema began to recycle these figures in recent films such as *Le fabuleux destin d'Amélie Poulain* (*Amélie*) (2001) and *La Môme* (*La vie en rose*) (2007), which became commercial hits beyond their national borders, a series of "Frenchness films" making use of similar figures emerged in the 1950s. As Vanessa Schwartz has argued,[7] these films—among them Jean Renoir's *French Cancan* (1954), Vincente Minelli's *Gigi* (1958), and Walter Lang's *Can-Can* (1960)—"represented 'France' at a particular time and place: Belle Époque Paris, which straddled two centuries and became the emblematic representation of France for movie audiences of the 1950s" (Schwartz, 20). Here it isn't Piaf, but an entire series of "turn-of-the-century clichés . . . the Can-Can, Moulin Rouge, Impressionist and Post-Impressionist paintings and palette, and commercial art posters," as well as the ubiquitous Maurice Chevalier referred to as one of "the biggest idiots of all the French" in *Breathless* (he and Louis Jourdan *both* starred in *Gigi* and *Can Can*), that "represented" France. Brigitte Bardot, who exploded on the international scene in Roger Vadim's *And God Created Woman* (1956) was the most emblematic of these French stereotypes and her constant presence on international screens marked the apogee of French film exports and of their international commercial success in the 1950s. "BB" was lauded by the New Wave as a symbol of youth and the star of a film that broke with the stilted cadences and outdated moralism of "daddy's cinema." To the French film establishment, as well as to the political establishment, Bardot was also exportable proof of France's ability to produce mass modern culture, since she emblematized not a France of the past, of Impressionism or the Moulin Rouge, but contemporary French youth. "BB" was also "modern" and,

7. Vanessa Schwartz, *It's So French! Hollywood, Paris, and the Making of Cosmopolitan Film Culture* (Chicago: University of Chicago Press, 2007).

as such, a precious exportable commodity for a nation that wanted to retain *grandeur* and relevance. However, the number of "BB films" that could be made was limited due to Bardot's private life, her attempted suicide, and her eventual withdrawal from cinema. The colorful, formulaic "BB" vehicles were soon replaced by the first films of the New Wave on the international market. And while these films also often portrayed contemporary "French youth," and constituted a formal revolution in film history, meeting with critical success that went well beyond the Hexagon, the very innovation they embodied made it impossible for them to break through as box office hits. The waning of "BB" films from the international scene thus also signaled the beginning of the end of commercial success for French cinema on the international marketplace as the first films of the New Wave began to appear. The issue was not France's ability to produce modern contemporary culture for export, as the success of the New Wave attests, but rather France's ability to produce contemporary, exportable, *commercially* successful mass culture. As Schwartz proposes:

> If Brigitte Bardot made the New Wave possible, the aesthetic triumph of the New Wave around the world replaced the middle-brow slick color films of Bardot as the carriers of Frenchness. The embrace of the New Wave by intellectuals in France and abroad guaranteed France a major role in the development of film "art." By the end of the New Wave, French films had transformed into a luxury item, and "popular" French film more or less disappeared outside the Hexagon. (Schwartz, 145)

Here Schwartz makes a distinction that is simultaneously simple and crucial: between "popular" French films, those "slick color films" starring Brigitte Bardot in the 1950s, and those more rarefied films she labels "luxury items." Rephrased, the opposition is between films that were widely distributed and, by extension, commercially successful, and those that were not. In other words, "highbrow" or "intellectual" or "experimental" French films—ostensibly, those of the New Wave—may be formally innovative and push back the frontiers of cinema, but they do not (or seldom do) meet with "popular"—that is commercial—success outside France.

French films seem to be caught between the following two classifications: those that, through their representation of a France of clichés manage to break through the threshold of international commercial viability, and those that are for "the happy few." Claude Lelouch, the director of the international box office hit *Un homme et une femme* (*A Man and a Woman*), which won the Oscar for Best Foreign Film in 1966 as well as the Golden Palm at the Cannes Film Festival and a host of other awards that year, made it a point in a subsequent (and commercially unsuccessful) film to lampoon the "art film" and its lack of popular appeal. In a scene from Lelouch's 1972 *La bonne annèe* (*The Happy New Year*), we see that arch-icon of French gangster films, Lino Ventura, playing a bank robber who has come to Cannes to pull off a jewelry heist, solidly sitting at an elegant and decidedly "highbrow" Christmas Eve dinner given by his love interest in the film, the well-read owner of an antique shop. Ventura and his sidekick are the "lowbrows" to the love interest's "intellectual" guests. When the conversation turns to film, which is supposedly an effort to bring the pair of quiet gangsters into the flow of things, but in fact is just another means of making them feel inadequate, Ventura has to repeatedly answer "no" to another guest's increasingly insistent questions about his having seen this or that film, all by "art" directors of the period. Politely exasperated, at one point the cinephile asks: "But surely you've seen *A Man and a Woman!!?*" (that *popular* box office hit, the film that *everyone* has seen). In the ensuing silence, the (diegetic) classical music that had been playing during the dinner becomes the only sound heard before another of the "intellectuals" quips: "Maybe you would have preferred the accordion?" The obvious targets are the "lowbrow gangsters." However, violence is averted as they politely leave, while the "highbrow intellectuals" are swiftly kicked out by the hostess who, preferring "hunted men and victims," ends up in bed with Ventura in the very next scene. Throughout the dinner scene, Lelouch is obviously settling accounts with the New Wavers, who did not count him as one of their own, and, beyond the direct allusion to films, he selects an archetypal sign of French popular culture to make his point: the accordion. While the cinephiles may listen to classical music, the accordion, with its echoes of *guinguettes* and Montmartre and *chansons*, metonymically refers to an entire "popular" France of "petites gens" ("little people") that thirty years later would fill the screen in both Jean-Pierre Jeunet's *Le fabuleux destin d'Amélie Poulain* (2001) with its "retro-chic accordion soundtrack" (Vincendeau) and, more recently, in *La Môme* (2007), where, unsurprisingly, in this biopic about Edith Piaf, the accordion reigns supreme.

Professional film critics and academics have commented at length on the electronically enhanced—and sterilized—postcard Paris of *Amé-*

*lie.*[8] Ginette Vincendeau, for example, has made a list of the "petites gens de Paris" who inhabit Jeunet's film: "the weary *patronne,* an irascible customer, a weepy concierge, a hypochondriac tobacconist, a cantankerous grocer, a mysterious old man, as well as one or two new types such as the sassy porn-video shop assistant and the photo-booth repairman." As for Amélie's peregrinations, they take her through some of those very icons that France had attempted to "copyright" in its initial encounter with the consolidating power of the American film industry after World War I—Notre Dame, the Sacré Coeur, and so on, as well as through the "quaintness" of Parisian rooftops, cobble stone streets, and cafés. *Amélie's* incredible commercial success in France as well as at the international box office, its ability to break through that threshold of "mega hit," is directly linked to its ability to portray these clichés: things are "set right," the burnished France that remains as a set of stereotypes is the one that is recognizable beyond the passage of time and the vicissitudes of history. Clichés sell better because they simultaneously freeze, simplify, and confirm our idealized take on the world, and Jeunet's own declaration in this regard is symptomatic: "We live at a time when there are no longer big political (or otherwise) ideals and to be able to focus on small pleasures, I think that's great" (quoted in Vincendeau). In this regard, *Amélie,* which was said by one critic to represent a "Euro-Disney Paris" indeed shares with a certain American cinema an ability to both idealize and infantilize, which are key to the recipe of "entertainment" and, it follows, box office success.

In Olivier Dahan's *La Môme,* that voice heard rising over the rubble of a bombed-out Normandy town in 1944 by a group of GIs in Spielberg's *Saving Private Ryan* takes on epic dimensions, as befits a legend and one of the most transnational figures of "Frenchness," Edith Piaf. Here again, a French film's visibility and commercial success—its star, Marion Cotillard, won the Oscar for Best Actress in 2008, the first French actress to win that award since Simone Signoret in 1959, and it has done brisk business worldwide—is directly related to its representation of archetypal figures. And while its "look" does not share the airbrushed quality of *Amélie,* it nevertheless thrives on its subject's metonymic ability to become Paris and, by extension, France. The film

8. Among others, see Dudley Andrew, "Amélie, or Le Fabuleux Destin du Cinéma Français," *Film Quarterly* 57/3 (Spring, 2004): 34–46, and Ginette Vincendeau, "Café Society," http://www.bfi.org.uk/sightandsound/feature/15

opens with the by now essentialized image of Piaf alone on a stage, her face a pasty white, her lips bright red, standing in front of the microphone, dressed in black, the spotlight focused on her. We are in New York on February 16, 1956, and she's about to collapse. While the film then takes us on a jagged chronological tour from 1919 Belleville to Piaf's final performance at the Oympia—with the resulting melodramatic impact of her finally singing her cult hit, "Je ne regrette rien"— it scrupulously and exclusively avoids the Occupation years, or the "Dark Years" (1940–1944), eliding a period that was no less important in Piaf's life and career than the other years covered in the film. Dahan's focus, it is fair to say, is not History but Piaf, the Life of Piaf, the lyrical presentation of an icon, not a historical figure. The film has its share of urchins, narrow streets, and cafés, even if, this time, as opposed to the Montmartre of *Amélie,* the lighting hovers between chiaroscuro and a range we might call "raw poetic," with its bright colors suffused in sepia. Both registers are used in one of the film's most cloying frames *illustrating* or visually replicating a statement made just before by none other than Marlene Dietrich in her own soulful voice to the gushing Piaf in an elegant restaurant after a performance: "I haven't been to Paris in ages. But tonight, when you were singing, I was there, with its streets, beneath its sky; *your voice is the soul of Paris.* You took me on a journey, you made me cry" (emphasis mine). Dahan follows with a shot of the Paris sky at sunset, with the Eiffel Tower in the background, its silhouette dark against the orange to deep blue sky while, in the foreground, a gigantic head of Piaf in glossy black and white completes the association: Piaf *is* the Eiffel Tower, which is Paris, and, by extension, France. Amélie-Montmartre-France, and Brigitte Bardot-of-the-bikini-France—who had been dubbed the "Eyeful Tower" in the American media in the 1950s—belong to the same series of essentialized, metonymic figures that recapture for film audiences an entire culture, if not in its former glory, at least in a cliché- and kitsch-driven familiarity that makes "France" absolutely recognizable and thus marketable to film audiences worldwide.

In the end, the issue is not France's ability to produce films that are commercially successful within its borders. These films are made annually and are overwhelmingly, as we would suspect, of the "popular" rather than of the "art house" category and belie any idea of France exclusively as a locus of "high brow" films: Patrick Leconte's *Les bronzés 3* (2006) broke the record for best debut for films of all nationalities in

France, while Dany Boon's *Bienvenue chez les Chtis* (2008) was the most successful movie of all time in the Hexagon, surpassing James Cameron's international blockbuster, *Titanic*. (On the "art house" front, however, Bruno Dumont's *Flandres*, the 2006 winner of the Cannes film festival's Grand Prix, sold barely 80,000 tickets in French theaters, and Benoît Jacquot's *The Untouchable*, which won best actress prize at Venice the same year, sold an abysmal 35,000 tickets nationally). Neither is the issue France's ability to produce films that can be exported internationally and meet with either critical or commercial success, as attested by the acclaim bestowed on the New Wave, and the box office returns on a number of French films over the past six decades (from the "BB films" to *Amélie*), but, rather, France's ability to *consistently* produce and export commercially successful films that are neither "Hollywoodian" nor, as we have explored in this essay, films that recycle a "certain idea of France."

Is there a "third way"? Is there another "recipe"? This is obviously not a question that has to be faced by American cinema, which is both "Hollywoodian" *and* exports a "certain idea" of its culture: *this* national cinema is the meeting place of a particular way of "making movies" (the recipe of global *spectacularity* referred to above) and of a country that is the paradigmatic nation of the age of globalization. Figuratively, the Manhattan skyline (both before and after 9/11) sets the pace, and routinely dominates the international box office in a way that the Eiffel Tower, the Taj Mahal, the Brandenburg Gate, or the Acropolis do not (unless we are watching one of those, usually Hollywood-produced, "international thrillers," one of the "Bourne franchise" movies, to name just one example, in which an entire series of these "international" sites appear as background to the adventures of the—usually English-speaking—hero). It isn't that the Manhattan skyline is any less reductive or essentialized than the Eiffel Tower, but that it metonymically partakes of a culture perceived as *the* planetary present, of the actively *actual*. Hollywood films emanate and gain momentum from the widely and incessantly disseminated popular culture of the U.S., even as we hear talk of the "end of the American Empire" or of a "post-American world" (Fareed Zakaria). A combination of factors has perpetuated the dominance acquired by this American cinema since World War I: the increasing geopolitical clout of the U.S., its "sharp commercial practices" (from early "block booking" to today's market dumping), the unabashed practice of filmmaking as business and entertainment, production values and narrative techniques that result in the "polished veneer" (de Grazia) American films have acquired since the end of World War I and which has only been made more glossy with time. As a result, the stories American cinema tells and its way of telling these stories, its way of making films, *appear to be,* but to a large extent also impose themselves as being "what the people of [all countries] want to see," as Jack Valenti declared. For the massive audiences it takes to create an international box office hit, to partake of American culture, of its cinema in this instance, is thus to partake of the "now and the (post) modern," just as to speak English is to partake of the lingua franca of the international, hyper-commodified Disneyworld of post-modernity in which we are not beckoned to think, but rather to join in the shopping spree of the supposedly postideological global pleasure dome. In this context, French cinema, with its own narrative forms and its own stories, appears singularly "local," and therein is the core of the issue. We should, however, be careful not to interpret "local" as "parochial," "passé," "self-indulgent," or "high brow and boring" (all in one breath) as French cinema has sometimes been labeled recently,[9] but to consider instead the network of factors examined in this essay that has led to the present situation. A "third way" might only arise as the very nationality of films (including American films), whether their figures or narrative forms, becomes indeterminate, signaling the waning of a global paradigm dominated by American cinema. In the meantime, the recycling of globally recognizable figures, or alignment along the norms of commercial/Hollywood American cinema may well be the only ways for national cinemas to systematically break through that threshold of international commercial success. This may seem a rather dire pronouncement, ostensibly conflating as it does success and commercialism; but, after all, this essay has focused on the capacity for a national cinema, in this case French cinema, to produce internationally and commercially successful films, and not on the intrinsic value of any given national cinema, whether it be French, Indian, Chinese . . . or American. Two related and underlying questions, questions that were never quite broached here, but nevertheless inform the entire essay, may well serve as a (temporary) conclusion: is that old opposition between "commercial cinema" and "another type of cinema" still valid? And: can that "other" cinema—whether Chinese, Indian, French, or American—ever be internationally, commercially successful?

9. Among others, see Angelique Chrisafis, "Cinema in France: It's oui to rom-coms and non to art house as cinéphiles die out," *The Guardian* (January 29, 2007).

# CATHERINE PORTUGES

# French Women Directors Negotiating Transnational Identities

The cinematic representation of transnational processes over the past decade has engaged a number of women filmmakers in France, extending earlier discourses of national cinema and postcoloniality. As Françoise Lionnet and Shu-mei Shih have argued, "The transnational . . . can be conceived as a space of exchange and participation wherever processes of hybridization occur and where it is still possible for cultures to be produced and performed without necessary mediation by the center."[1]

The fiftieth anniversary of the French New Wave, launched by young directors to protest the hegemonic filmmaking practices of a studio-based system, constitutes a point of departure for many of these filmmakers and a frame of reference for this essay.[2] For just as New Wave filmmakers such as Jean-Luc Godard, François Truffaut, Agnès Varda, Eric Rohmer, Claude Chabrol, and Jacques Rivette used the jump cut, the tracking shot, real-time long takes, and camera movements to call attention to the cinematic apparatus in a provocative manifesto, so, too, do these transnational directors propose innovations worthy of attention.

Borrowing from avant-garde, independent, and commercial film practices of French and European cinema, and combining them with the specificities of diasporan filmmaking, French women filmmakers are calling into question the validity of both national cinema and cultural identity as assumed or fixed representational concepts. A number

1. *Minor Transnationalism*, ed. Françoise Lionnet and Shu-mei Shih (Durham and London: Duke University Press, 2005), 1–21.

2. See Antoine de Baecque, *La nouvelle vague. Portrait d'une jeunesse* (Paris: Flammarion, 1998).

**YFS 115,** *New Spaces for French and Francophone Cinema,* ed. James F. Austin,
© 2009 by Yale University.

of these bilingual and bicultural directors, themselves transnational products of Mediterranean and African contexts trained in Western universities and film schools, practice a form of filmmaking that resists authoritarian hegemonic discourses. Although they do not necessarily constitute a movement, their filmmaking strategies similarly gesture at once toward and away from the cultures of their primary affiliation, implicating the viewer in a nomadic trajectory from a context familiar to Western audiences toward a less familiar space, and back again. Traversing these increasingly permeable geographical and interpersonal boundaries, such films call into question hierarchies of power that inscribe immigrant female others within the parameters of a "host" nation—in this case, France.[3]

The directors considered here, all of whom work in both documentary and fiction genres, suggest only part of the vibrant filmmaking community in contemporary French cinema whose achievements further attest, should such confirmation still be necessary, to the innovative contributions of women to moving image practice since the earliest days of silent cinema. Likewise, cinema itself has, from its inception, been a transnational art and industry, from pre-narrative cinema, to international silent film and the avant-garde.[4] Disrupting and widening the horizons of contemporary visual culture, Claire Denis, Chantal Akerman, Josiane Balasko, Catherine Breillat, Aline Isserman, Diane Kurys, Tonie Marshall, Brigitte Roüan, Vera Belmont, Coline Serreau, and Agnès Varda all produced new work in the 1990s, exploring issues of national identity and ethnicity, sexuality and gender, and marginality and displacement. Other noteworthy French co-productions have been located on the transnational margins of filmmaking, such as very recent work from the younger generation of women filmmakers including Isild Le Besco's *Charly* (2007); Zina Modiano's *Vie privée* (*Private Life*) (2005), Lola Doillon's *Et toi t'es sur qui?* (*Just About Love?*, 2007), Celina Sciamma's *Naissance des pieuvres* (*Water Lilies*, 2007), Mia Hansen-Love's *Tout est pardonné* (*All is Forgiven*, 2007), Emmanuelle Cuau's *Très bien, merci* (*Very Well, Thank You*, 2007), and Marjane Satrapi's *Persepolis* (2007).

Claire Denis, a leading innovator of this generation who had worked

3. See Carrie Tarr, "The Porosity of the Hexagon: Border Crossings in Contemporary French Cinema," *Studies in European Cinema* 4/1 (May 2007): 7–20.

4. See *Cinema and the Invention of Modern Life*, ed. Vanessa R. Schwartz and Leo Charney (University of California Press, 1995).

previously with a number of New Wave directors, pays homage to one of her mentors in her 1990 documentary *Cinéma de notre temps: Jacques Rivette, le veilleur* (Cinema of Our Time: Jacques Rivette, the Watchman). As a French West African woman with a profound understanding of contrasting continental geopolitics, Denis was also inspired by the work of the younger generation of filmmakers who shared her commitment to the motif of foreignness, otherness, and strangeness. In *Beau travail* (1999), one of the few films by women directors to focus on masculinity and the male body in an intimate, personal mediation, Denis contemplates the erotic and professional attachments among men in the French Foreign Legion in a former French colony. In *Beau travail*, Denis again demonstrates the feel for African landscape evident in her first feature film, *Chocolat* (1988), where scenes of domestic life take place at a remove from public space between African servants and *pied-noir* families, as in the powerful connection between Aimée, a white woman in her twenties, and Protée, her Cameroonian servant. As her career has progressed, she has determinedly followed her own path, at times eschewing narrative for the pleasures of the visual. In *35 Rhums* (*35 Shots of Rum*, 2007), Denis traces a whole community of characters from France's working underclass, anchored by a father–daughter relationship, framing them within a milieu that defines their aspirations yet circumscribes their lives.

Working in co-production and through independent circuits beyond conventional structures of production, distribution, and exhibition, these filmmakers are charting the presence of otherness in contemporary representational modes, incorporating in the process autobiographical elements that cross boundaries of genre, combining fiction and nonfiction, as well as animation and experimental formats. By chronicling the multilayered dispersals, exiles, and migrations of diasporic populations, including personal narratives of their own families and their *entourages*, they problematize integration, solidarity, and hybrid identities. As I have suggested elsewhere, the mise-en-scène of the earlier generation of directors "destabilizes hegemonic ideas of nationality, sexuality, and the family"[5] in which the *Hexagone* is figured

5. Catherine Portuges, "*Le colonial féminin:* Women Directors Interrogate French Cinema," *Cinema, Colonialism, Postcolonialism: Perspectives from the French and Francophone World*, ed. Dina Sherzer (Austin: University of Texas Press, 1996), 80–102. I propose in this article a "second wave" of films directed by women, examining female subjectivity and women's roles in the colonial past to explore history, memory, and family.

as a multicultural zone of intergenerational protagonists and immigrant populations.

In a career that spans nearly six decades, Agnès Varda, now in her eightieth year and one of the major figures of postwar cinema (her first feature, *La pointe courte*, 1954, is a precursor of the French New Wave), has remained an active inspiration for generations of women directors. She has, moreover, controlled production and distribution through her own company, Ciné Tamaris. In her view, being a female filmmaker " . . . means separating yourself from your mirror and the image that society proposes for you, leaving the kitchen, going outside, looking at others, choosing and negotiating with difficulties and contradictions."[6] In *Les glaneurs et la glaneuse* (2000), Varda implicates herself as a documentary filmmaker in the practice of gleaning, considered transnational for the way it circumvents social and economic structures. Traversing France from the north to La Beauce, passing through the Jura, Provence, the eastern Pyrénées, the Parisian suburbs and the Montreuil flea-market in Paris, the film distinguishes gleaning from foraging, pilfering, scavenging, rummaging, collecting, and recovering, as practiced by segments of the population for whom it has become a way of life.[7]

In her most autobiographical documentary to date, *Les plages d'Agnès* (2008), Varda takes the international metaphor of beaches as a point of departure, narrating in her own voice a "self-portrait via photographs, film clips, and some surprising encounters,"[8] weaving photographs, vintage footage, scenes from her films, and present-day sequences into a memorable voyage through her lifelong negotiation with otherness, confronting the joy of creativity and the pain of personal loss, death, and aging. Hers is a singular journey across cultures, played out against the postwar explosion of cultural expression in France. Following her intermittent appearance in front of the camera in *The Gleaners*, here for the first time Varda appears more fully realized as herself. Exploring her beginnings as a stage photographer working under Jean Vilar at the Festival d'Avignon and then as the official

6. Agnès Varda, interview in *Studio Magazine* 154 (March 2000). All translations in this article my own. I am grateful to Agnès Varda for sharing her thoughts on this subject with me on several occasions, particularly in the context of the Toronto International Film Festival, September 2000.

7. See Portuges, "*The Gleaners and I* (*Les Glaneurs et la Glaneuse*) by Agnès Varda," *The American Historical Review* 106/1 (Feb. 2001): 305–306.

8. Personal interview with Agnès Varda, Toronto Film Festival, September 8, 2008.

photographer for the Théâtre National Populaire, her early filmmaking as part of the *Nouvelle Vague,* her life with Jacques Demy, her feminism, her coverage of China in 1957, the Cuban Revolution in 1962, and her experience in the United States during the years of the Vietnam War, Varda exemplifies the intersections of transnationalism and gender within cinematic practice.[9]

Echoing Varda's practice as an independent filmmaker, a younger generation of women directors is also engaged in negotiating questions of difference and otherness. Following the trajectories of protagonists located in metropolitan French urban space as well as in regional and rural settings, they propose a remapping of cultural formations by gesturing toward the transnational, the diasporan, the globalized, the creolized, and by posing cultural, religious, gendered, and ethical questions.[10] Their explorations of intimacy recall those of Varda and Claire Denis, as well as Brigitte Roüan, who examined colonial spaces of private life among women in *Outremer* (1990), with its narrative of three sisters living with their families in Algeria during the final years of French colonial rule. Set in the late 1940s, the film's opening scenes depict French colonial life as a coddled existence in a semi-tropical paradise before the nationalist uprising that eventually drove a million Europeans to leave the country. The director, who also co-wrote the film and who plays one of the sisters, proceeds gradually to deconstruct the mechanisms of their cruel frivolity, sense of entitlement, and racism through a feminist lens.

Another narrative of sisters that demonstrates the power of cinema to make visible and public what is otherwise hidden and private, unseen or unsaid, Karin Albou's first feature, *La petite Jérusalem* (*Little Jerusalem,* 2005) is set in 2002 in the wake of the second Intifada in the Parisian *banlieue* of Sarcelles known as "*la petite Jérusalem.*"[11] According to the director, herself from a North African Sephardic background, "People think that Jews live in the wealthy center of Paris, but

9. Special thanks to Agnès Varda for the opportunity to speak with her after the premiere of *Les plages d'Agnès* (2008, Toronto International Festival).

10. I wish to thank Mark Reid, François Lionnet, and Sylvie Blum for inviting me to present my research at earlier stages of this essay for the Society for Cinema and Media Studies ("A (re)New(ed) French Cinema of Tricolor: Beur, Blanc, Black"), the UCLA Mellon Seminar in French and Francophone Studies, and the France-Florida Institute, University of Florida Gainesville, respectively.

11. 2002 also marked the fortieth anniversary of the end of the Algerian War of Independence. I thank Mary Lawrence Test for her astute comments and suggestions on this essay.

a part of the Jewish population lives with Muslim and African immigrants in low-income suburbs and *cités*. Many *banlieue* films deal with
other populations—Antillais, *beurs*, blacks, Arabs—but not Jews.[12] So
I thought it was more interesting to place my story in this suburb, one
of the most important, emblematic centers of North African immigration to France."[13] Here, in an ultra-Orthodox Sephardic Tunisian
family's cramped apartment, Laura, a student, rejects both her sister
Mathilde's obsession with Halachic law and her mother's interpretation of Orthodoxy, preferring instead the secular rigors of Kantian
philosophy and compelled by her attraction to Djamel, an Algerian co-
worker. Prompted by recent anti-Semitic attacks on a nearby synagogue, Ariel (her brother-in-law) orders Laura to suspend her evening
walks in the *quartier* (neighborhood), a ritual she had been observing
in honor of Kant's daily promenade along an unvarying itinerary, *le
chemin du philosophe* (the philosopher's walk). While Laura refuses to
obey Ariel, Djamel's Muslim family is equally opposed to his involve-
ment with a Jewish woman, and when they insist that she convert,
Djamel ends the relationship. In a key sequence set in Djamel's family
home, his father asks him, in Arabic, why he could not have found a
suitable Muslim partner: "Laura is not an Arab name!" (Nor for that
matter is it a Jewish name, but rather is of Greek origin).

In *La petite Jérusalem*, extreme close-up shots of Laura—her face,
hands, hair, and legs—create an atmosphere of intimacy and mute contestation in the film's opening sequence as she dresses for the day while
reading a prayer book. Insisting on her physical presence yet without
an eroticizing gaze, the director provocatively cross-cuts Laura's ritual
with shots of Ariel, alone in his bedroom, absorbed in his morning ritual,[14] contrasting her budding sexuality with his devotion to religion.

12. An important precursor is *La haine* (*Hate*) (Kassovitz, 1995). Its Criterion (2007)
DVD release includes interviews with sociologists on the *banlieues* and a feature-length
documentary with news footage of the riots that inspired the film.

13. Personal interview with Karin Albou, Walter Reade Theater, New York City, February 2005. Albou's second feature, *Aïd el-Kébir* (Grand Prix, Clermont-Ferrand Film
Festival) focuses on Algeria, her parents' homeland. At the end of *La petite Jérusalem*,
the Sephardic family prepares to emigrate to Israel, trading their Paris flat for a four-story
house, fantasized in the children's game of Lego. As Ella Shohat has argued in "Zionism
from the Standpoint of its Jewish Victims," the imagined community of their dreams is
known to be less welcoming to Sephardic Jews than to Ashkenazim. See Ella Shohat,
"Sephardim in Israel: Zionism from the Standpoint of its Jewish Victims," *Social Text*
19–20 (Autumn 1988): 1–35. See also Esther Benbassa, *The Jews of France* (Princeton:
Princeton University Press, 2001).

14. These images recall the opening of *Kadosh* (1999) directed by Amos Gitai, which

Within this mise-en-scène of Jewish communal space, *La petite Jéru-salem* positions gender, female desire, and the relationship of two sisters at the heart of its argument. The alternating dynamic between private and public stages the scene for Mathilde and Ariel's inability to experience sexual intimacy, and the infidelity to which he is presumably driven by his wife's inhibitions. Two sequences set in the *mikvah*, the Orthodox Jewish women's ritual baths, focus on Mathilde's slender body and long, dark hair as the object of the camera's intense gaze; there, in that private women's space, she begins to reconcile her commitment to Orthodoxy with Talmudic acceptance of erotic pleasure within traditional marriage as she engages in conversation with the *tukerin*,[15] the woman in charge of the *mikvah*. Visually and discursively, the sacred is linked with the profane, gesturing at—inspired by Kant—the possibility of an eventual synthesis. Similarly, the film explores the contested terrain of potential intimacy between Jews and Muslims in a series of erotically charged shots of Laura and Djamel changing into work clothes, standing back to back in the locker room of the institution where they are employed as custodians. The camera's gaze unflinchingly observes their sense of danger, discomfort, and transgressive attraction, which culminates in a scene of passionate connection.

Exploring the interplay between sexuality and religion, *La petite Jérusalem* proposes the possibility of linking a kind of cultural intimacy with historical memory. It is tempting to understand the complex relationship between Laura and Djamel as evoking the lost intimacy of an idealized North African past. Contemporary migrant subjects, Laura and Djamel are marked as originating in different nations as well as religions—his family is from Algeria; hers, from Tunisia. What begins as a questioning of the ostensible differences between Jews and Muslims ultimately gives way to an examination of the more powerful forces of nationality and gender. When Laura finds a talisman under her bed, and when her mother uses a folk remedy to cure her daughter's depression, one is reminded of popular Maghrebi beliefs and practices

---

also concerns two sisters in an Orthodox family and links religion and sexual passion in the Jerusalem of Israel, beginning with a close-up of an Hasidic Jew at morning prayers. *Kadosh* takes place entirely within a Hassidic milieu (Mea Shearim) and presents a harsh critique of the gender politics of religious orthodoxy.

15. Yiddish, from *tukn*, to immerse; in Hebrew, *balanit*, feminine form of *balan*, bathhouse keeper. Alone with the bather during these sessions, she may serve as an informal psychological counselor (*Jewish Daily Forward*, 18 January 2008).

ascribed both to Muslims and Jews. When their Tunisian mother shows Mathilde a photo taken at La Goulette, the port of Tunis, twenty years earlier, we can assume that she emigrated around 1982, although no explanatory material is offered for that history, nor reasons provided for her husband's death. The photograph invites the viewer to reflect on connections rather than differences between Jews and Muslims, recalling Ferid Boughedir's *Un été à La Goulette* (*A Summer in La Goulette*, 1995), set during the summer of 1966 in the small beach resort near Tunis shortly before the Arab-Israeli war where three sixteen-year-old girls—Meriem the Muslim, Gigi the Jew and Tina the Catholic—vow to lose their virginity at the same time with a boy from a religion other than their own.

Unlike the restored intimacy between Mathilde and Ariel, the relationship between Laura and Djamel is doomed to failure: its emblems are Djamel's scars, presumably acquired in a violent attack against him as a journalist in Algeria, where, as an independent intellectual, he had begun a book on the first Arab woman Sufi poet. In the most literal sense, the scars on his body re-evoke the violence that has claimed more than 150,000 lives since 1991. As a journalist critical of religion, Djamel had been targeted by armed Islamist groups, the film seems to imply, and had fled, without legal standing and as an undocumented refugee, to France. In a French context, the scars are also emblematic of the torture and violence perpetrated by the French army and police during the Algerian War of Independence—a highly charged topic that has reemerged in the last few years in a number of French productions.[16] Finally, Djamel's marked body and his status as an undocumented refugee recall current French debates over the rights of undocumented migrants (*sans papiers*),[17] and may also refer to the torture in

16. Michel Haneke's 2005 film *Caché* (*Hidden*) explores the terrain of France's repressed colonial past with haunting power; here, Djamel says he was "obligé de me cacher" (obliged to hide).

17. Recent films such as Rachid Bouchareb's Franco-Algerian-Moroccan co-produced feature *Indigènes* (*Days of Glory*, 2006) revisit the colonial history of France and Algeria. Philippe Faucon's *Dans la vie* (*Two Ladies*, 2007) is set in contemporary France in a working-class neighborhood where three female protagonists (Jews and Muslims) negotiate their lives together. In *Algérie, histoires à ne pas dire* (*Unspoken Stories*) (Lledo, 2007), four Muslim Algerians consider what might have been had the million refugees who fled Algeria after independence in 1962—Arab, Berber and European, Muslim, Christian and Jew—been able to remain. *L'esquive* (*Games of Love and Chance*) (Kechiche, 2003) foregrounds youth from the projects whose intrigues are interwoven with a staging of Marivaux's *Les jeux de l'amour et du hasard*. *La graine et le mulet* (*The Secret of the Grain* or *Couscous*) (Kechiche, 2007) portrays Slimane, an older shipyard

Abu Ghraib, Guantánamo Bay, and elsewhere. Like films of the New Wave, *La pétite Jerusalem* offers no seamless closure. The political and personal significance of Djamel's past is left unresolved, for he disappears from the narrative before the end of the film; the final shot of Laura frames her alone, riding the metro escalator in her neighborhood.

That the camera focuses only rarely on such moments in public space, beyond the domestic confines of the home, further underscores the film's status as a chamber piece, a *vase clos*, particularly in view of the ways in which the world outside inflect the narrative. For despite the location of Sarcelles, and the fact that the Jewish family members speak both French and Hebrew together, the French nation is evoked only tangentially, as in a scene set in Laura's philosophy class, when the professor asks her to elaborate on Kant's concept of freedom, and in exterior shots of the *cité*'s multiracial population on the street and in the metro. The most notable and dramatic absence, however, is that of the Arab community—in particular, the Muslim Algerians figured through the character of Djamel.[18] The Jewish protagonists occupy the foreground, while the Muslims remain in the background; the viewer is led to assume that what transpires in this largely invisible, contested zone between the communities leads to the Jewish family's ultimate decision to make *aliyah* (immigration of Jews to Israel), driven primarily by an unprovoked attack on Ariel during a soccer match. Yet the historical and political contexts are figured only as a shadowy backdrop, one that the filmmaker interpolates without offering the evidence that might more fully explain its importance.[19]

*La petite Jérusalem* raises urgent questions of religious interpreta-

---

worker, who engages rival families in a project to transform an old, decrepit boat into a restaurant specializing in couscous with fish.

18. The resulting asymmetry is discernible in the film's publicity, which focuses on images of the romantic couple constituted by the Tunisian Jewish woman and the Algerian Muslim man.

19. Laura tells Djamel's relatives that she was born in Djerba, an island off the southeast coast of Tunisia, "near the synagogue," one of the most venerable Jewish communities in the Mediterranean (see Lucette Valensi and Abraham Udovitch, *The Last Arab Jews: The Communities of Jerba, Tunisia* [Chur: Harwood Academic, 1984]) where, in 1997, a suicide bomber detonated a truck bomb at the synagogue. Albou has stated that she purposely set the film in 2002 when there were anti-Semitic attacks on schools in Sarcelles and on a synagogue in neighboring Goussainville. In fact, this violence occurred after the second Intifada, and some have argued a connection between the two events. While the film implies that masked Arabs are the aggressors against Ariel on the soccer field, some historians suggest that it would be more likely for them to be neo-Nazi skinheads, which is not an option within the film's logic.

tion, interethnic conflict, and gender identity in multicultural metropolitan France; its allusive references to Muslims and Jews engage both communities in attenuated fashion, leaving the viewer with a somewhat elusive sense of what both unites and separates them. The film's undercurrent of female sexuality reinforces connections among women whose images are de-eroticized by the sheer ordinariness of their gestures, yet at the same time embellished by the lighting of cinematographer Laurent Brunet. *La petite Jérusalem* suggests, finally, in an unwavering statement of feminine empowerment, that a sense of self may also be inextricably linked to religious and intellectual practice, leaving the viewer to reflect on the gendered consequences of erotic violence, the violent eroticism of visual intimacy, and the legacy of colonialism.

Algerian-born director Dominique Cabrera's first fiction feature, *L'autre côté de la mer* (*The Other Shore*, 1996), also belongs to the socially and economically conscious films of the 1990s.[20] For just as *La petite Jérusalem* references interethnic conflict in the Middle East, so, too, do Cabrera's urban spaces evoke, albeit indirectly, terrorism in North Africa. Evoking discourses on Islamism and the nation, she, too, brings to the fore the status and treatment of undocumented and homeless populations and the consequences of Islamic fundamentalism, both in Algeria and France. Situated in the postmodern cultural geography of the Parisian urban zone, *L'autre côté de la mer* engages its transnational imagined (and real) communities in an essay on space and social identity by inserting its characters in locations made all the more intimately resonant in that they are often entered via a hand-held camera from the cinematographer's point of view.

*L'autre côté de la mer*'s fictional narrative takes place in the present, and Cabrera's commitment to emphasizing the diversity of contemporary Franco-Algerian experiences and representations underscores its multiple points of view and perspectives. The "other shore" of the title can, of course, depending on one's perspective, be either Algeria or France. The film's protagonist, George Montero (played by Claude Brasseur), an Algerian-born Frenchman (*pied noir*) and proprietor of an olive oil company in Oran, chooses to remain in Algeria, yet continues

20. For example, Bruno Dumont's *La vie de Jésus* (1997); Jean-François Richet's *Ma 6-t va craquer* (1997); Matthieu Kassowitz's *La haine*; Claire Denis' *Nénette et Boni*; Sylvie Verheyde's *Un frère* (1997), Robert Guédiguian's *Marius et Jeannette* (1997); and Karim Dridi's *Bye-Bye* (1995).

to call France "*la métropole*" even after Algeria's 1962 independence. Arriving in Paris for the first time, more than thirty years after many of his compatriots, he finds his countrymen everywhere, yet seems unable to see or hear them, or to heed their advice. Suffering from blurred vision, literally and figuratively, and in denial about his own status as an alien in France, he is immediately ready to return to Oran. Yet he must quickly plan the cataract surgery that prompted his journey, and it is in the operating room that clarity of vision becomes an existential trope. The eye, isolated through surgical instrumentation, embodies Montero's character not only as a harbinger of France's colonial past, but as a subject fully positioned in the present-day critical moment. The eye surgeon, played by Roschdy Zem, is an assimilated *beur* whose complicated identity owes a great deal to his rejection of his own Algerian roots. Eschewing *pied-noir* folkore—just as Claire Denis avoids Mediterranean stereotypes in her 1997 Marseilles-based film *Nénette et Boni*—this film's signature is warmly physical, even intimate, handheld documentary-style camerawork that privileges gesture over dialogue. Nontheless, words play a liberating role in revealing the protagonists' complicated history, a reminder that language can be the means by which continuity, rupture, and the consolidation of identities are articulated differently by male and female subjects. Though there are notably few Maghrebi women protagonists foregrounded in the film, their presence is nonetheless felt in the background and behind the scenes.[21]

Cabrera deploys a depth-of-focus technique that allows the background to remain secondary, integrating the multiple stories that constitute her scenario. Her objective is one of reconciliation, gesturing toward a conclusion in which her multigenerational protagonists might each possess a family photograph, an album that would serve to link families and individuals. Located discreetly in the margins of fiction, her documentary style unapologetically translates a complex vision of the world that positions the viewer within the frame of conflict.[22] A simple panorama of a garden chair and table, a camera that lingers mo-

21. Cabrera is herself a *pied noir* whose documentary style enables her to explore the various sites of Algerian emigration, the *lieux de mémoire* of the Algerian War that still resonate for Montero, the development of Islamic fundamentalism, and the evolution of *beur* identities. Numerous secondary characters appear in the course of the narrative, in quarrels among émigrés with contradictory political positions, from outright antagonism toward the French to mourning for the assassination of the much loved *raï* singer, Cheb Hasni. See Dominique Cabrera, interview with Françoise Audé and Y. Tobin, *Positif* 470, (April 2000): 35–39.

22. Aziza Boucherit, "Continuité, rupture et construction identitaires: analyse de

mentarily on the remains of a meal left outdoors in the sun, two or three shots of an olive grove in the Midi—scenes devoid of human presence that embody the materiality of the world those absent characters inhabit—are the vital links that weave together characters and settings. It is a scenario of desire, anchored in sensation, in which bodies combine, touch and reach out to one another. In this sense Cabrera may be seen as a materialist filmmaker whose poetry is the prose of the everyday; she rigorously avoids, however, the sentimentality that would threaten to neutralize its sphere of conflict.

The film's cinematographer, Hélène Louvart, traces movements of bodies and faces in search of diasporan zones and exilic voices, as in the masterfully shot sequence when Georges, after greeting his male friends (Arabs, *pieds-noirs,* and Jews) at the corner Parisian café, is reunited and reconciled with his relatives—a scene of little dialogue yet palpable emotion—for the first time since the end of the Algerian war. Along with Varda, Cabrera exhorts her audience to "grow . . . to grow through confrontation with others," marking *L'autre côté de la mer* as part of her project of reconciliation with otherness and difference, opening up the contested terrain of interethnic conflict, immigration, and deracination for further debate on France's colonial past. Cabrera's *oeuvre* seems to suggest that both documentary and fiction are equally valid manifestations of cinema, filmic ideas that are realized and concretized differently, yet always within a transnational framework.

Cabrera's subsequent "self-portrait," *Demain et encore demain— (Journal 1995) (Tomorrow and Again Tomorrow, 1997)* uses as a point of departure her description of herself as "an ordinary woman but a filmmaker." Cabrera explains her motivation for the film: "from January to September [1995] I decided to make a film of my life with my Hi8 camera. That year I loved a man and I filmed my mother. Like many other people I wondered whom I should vote for and where I should send my son to school; it was the same question, concerning our collective duty and triumphant liberalism."[23] These words recall those of Jean-Luc Godard, a powerful New Wave influence for Cabrera, "A man, merely a man, worth no more nor less than another," as well as those of Varda with regard to presenting oneself first as a filmmaker and only

---

discours d'immigrés maghrébins en France," *International Journal of the Sociology of Language* 190 (2008): 49–77.

23. In Agnès Calatayud, "An Ordinary Woman but a Film-maker: *Demain et encore demain* (1997)—Dominique Cabrera's Self-Portrait," *Studies in French Cinema* 1/1 (2001): 22–28.

then a woman. In *L'autre côté de la mer*, with its use of the hand-held camera to enter unobtrusively into the intimacy of daily conversations and gestures, the director raises the viewer's awareness of the indissoluble links among image, time, and narrative through the evolving relationships among Georges, Tarek, and their respective communities of different generations and cultures.

Set in a contrasting cultural, local, and affective register from the documentary-inspired work of Cabrera, the Moroccan-French co-production *Marock* (2005) is also an autobiographical meditation, albeit within a more commercial framework. Directed by Laïla Marrakchi, a Muslim married to a Sephardic Jew, educated at the University of Paris III where she received a DEA in Cinema and Audio-Visual Studies, the film is based on the director's own adolescent experience. Provocatively challenging taboos in traditional Muslim society, its main protagonist is Rita, a rebellious daughter of Casablanca's high society approaching the end of high school; she and her friends drink whiskey, smoke hashish, eat during Ramadan, and indulge in wild parties and romantic intrigue. Rita's youthful hedonism is troubled when she falls for the handsome daredevil Youri, a Jew. While her friends accept the affair, she must hide it from her parents and religiously conservative older brother. Marrakchi grew up in the world of the *jeunesse dorée* depicted in *Marock*, and in a Morocco renowned for religious tolerance and home to a centuries-old Jewish community. At the same time, she is cognizant that she is testing the boundaries of that world: "I knew in making this film that some things were going to cause discomfort, notably the love relationship between a young Muslim and young Jew. But for me, it is a symbol of peace and tolerance in a complicated world."

While anti-Jewish feeling has accompanied moments of political tension, and Jewish religious and community sites were targeted in bombing attacks in Casablanca in 2003, Moroccan Jews and Muslims have generally coexisted peacefully. Although secularists and liberals alike championed *Marock* as a step toward greater freedom of expression, debating it for months in print media and on the Internet, some considered it a "needless attack on Islamic values,"[24] taking particular offense at a scene in which Youri places his Star of David medallion around Rita's neck. Marrachki began to explore these transnational

---

24. The Malaysian Islamist newspaper *Al-Tajdid* called on readers to boycott the film, and the Islamist opposition Justice and Development Party demanded that it be banned.

themes in her earlier award-winning short film, *Lost Horizon*, which documents Abdeslam's final hours in Tangiers as he prepares to leave his lover, Rhimou, and his country for a supposedly better life on the other side of the horizon. As a clandestine voyager en route to Spain, he reminisces about Rhimou, his country, and what he is leaving behind.

A similar preoccupation with sexuality lies at the heart of another first feature by a young filmmaker, Nora Hamdi, who adapted her own first novel for the screen in *Des poupées et des anges* (2008). Born in Argenteuil and, like Cabrera, of Algerian descent, Hamdi's narrative, like that of Albou, focuses on the conflicts and solidarity among sisters. Lya, Chirine, and Inès live in a *cité* with a violent father who has given up on Chirine, his eldest daughter; only Lya is able to stand up to his anger. In Paris, Chirine meets a man who, identifying himself as an agent, promises her a successful modeling career. Thanks to Lya's unflinching lucidity, Chirine finally acknowledges that she is in fact becoming a prostitute. At this point Chirine meets Simon, a renowned advertising executive who takes her career in hand; Lya's uncompromising stance ultimately succeeds in reconciling the father with his daughters.

A former factory worker educated in night-school art courses, Hamdi is equally critical of both Paris and the *banlieue*, yet imbues her narrative with a hopeful optimism. Without compromise or pathos, she shows generosity toward the male characters, giving the father a second chance and appreciating the implicit humanity of Simon's admiration of both Chirine's beauty and her intelligence. While focusing on the family dynamics, the director's larger project implicitly questions the potential for reconciliation among the France of the *banlieues*, official Parisian images of its *quartiers difficiles*, and *la France profonde*.

Examining another family relationship, this time between a young widowed mother and her daughter, *Satin rouge* (Red Satin, 2002) is the début feature of Raja Amari, born in Tunis, who completed her studies in Paris's film school La FEMIS where she directed two short films. A Tunisian seamstress (played by the award-winning Palestinian actress Hiam Abass) takes an unlikely journey of self-discovery in this sumptuous and sensual film. Living out her routinized days, caring for her daughter and their apartment, knitting, sewing, and watching soap operas and romances on television, a young widow, Lilia, is unexpectedly drawn to an exotic nightclub netherworld of voluptuous belly dancers in the course of investigating a suspected liaison between her headstrong adolescent daughter, Salma, and a cabaret musician. Compelled by the dancers' intoxicating perfume, their kindness and alluring solidarity, Lilia embarks upon a new world populated by nocturnal pleasure-seekers, eventually becoming attracted to her daughter's young lover, Chakri. *Satin rouge* foregrounds the transformative power of female liberation, metaphorizing the erotic thrill and dramatic tension symbolized by the traditional belly dance. The film attracted critical and popular attention for its critique of misogyny and ageism by focusing on a woman in her forties who finds the courage to dance for the first time on stage in a cabaret frequented by her own daughters.

Amari herself trained as a belly dancer at the Conservatoire de Tunis, although she was forbidden to enter the cabaret near her family's apartment in Tunis. Returning to Tunis to shoot *Satin rouge*, she vowed to use that very space as a location and cast the dancers as actors in the film:

> We are bombarded by the media, and they show a certain image of the Arab world. What I want to do is bring a more subtle, more nuanced, vision of the world. Typically, in Arab films and Tunisian films you have a woman who is in conflict with society. . . . I didn't want that. That was not my subject, Lilia actually finds her freedom in the context of what I call social hypocrisy. She is involved in a society that is hypocritical in the sense that there are two worlds: the world of night and the world of day. What you do—what you really do—you do not show.[25]

These filmmakers' commitment to intergenerational and transnational representation is extended by the work of their *consoeur*, the documentary filmmaker Yamina Benguigui (who, with Rachid Bouchareb, director of *Indigènes*, founded the production company Bandits). Born in Lille to Algerian parents who came to France in the early 1950s, she experienced what she calls "not overt racism but observations. I was born in France, but would be asked: when are you going back? We were obviously [considered to be] there in transit."[26] Her first feature, *Inch'Allah dimanche* (2001), was inspired by her mother's generation of Algerian women, allowed by the French government in 1974 to rejoin their husbands who had been recruited to work thirty years earlier on the post-war reconstruction of France. At once a multifaceted fictionalized memoir and a tribute to these Maghrebi women im-

25. Raja Amari, "Interview: Self-Empowerment by Way of the Midriff; Raja Amari's *Satin Rouge*," interview by Kate Schultz, *Indiewire*, ⟨http://www.indiewire.com/people-int_Amari_Raja_020820⟩

26. Interview by Catherine Schwaab, *Paris Match* (19 October 2007).

migrants of the 1970s, the narrative is set in a transitional space—what Homi Bhabha has called a "third space"—one that transcends the binary polarities of cultural identity. In the wrenching opening sequence Zouina, the central character, bids farewell to her mother as her ship sets sail. Zouina travels with her three children and her mother-in-law to rejoin her husband Ahmed in northern France. Not unlike Laura's Sephardic mother in *La petite Jérusalem,* the dominating Aïcha mercilessly imposes her matriarchal traditions on the household.

Zouina nonetheless develops friendships with her French counterparts that enable her to more fully negotiate her own hybrid identity while longing for the culture she has left behind, as when she attempts to visit another Algerian woman who ultimately rejects her friendship, and later when she performs a traditional dance alone in her apartment, surrendering to the haunting melody and Arabic lyrics that evoke a lost homeland. Positioned between cultures, the female protagonists express their conflicts through gestures such as this that evoke other aural, visual, and sensual landscapes, constituting in this way a feminine visual space.[27] Zouina insists upon her legitimacy as a woman who integrates mobility, plurality, tradition, and modernity as she finds her way in multicultural France.[28] *Inch'Allah dimanche* exudes an ambiance of openness to difference and otherness, to reconciliation through dialogue, not unlike the atmosphere of *L'autre côté de la mer.* This feature was preceded by two documentaries, *Femmes d'Islam* (Women of Islam, 1994), and *Mémoires d'immigrés: l'héritage maghrébin* (*Immigrant Memories,* 1997). In combination with *Inch'Allah dimanche,* they form a triptych of stories of the fate of two generations of Maghrebi immigration: the men who left North Africa to forge their way in the "paradise" of France; the lives of the women who came to join their struggling husbands; and the children whose identity is blurred and forgotten as a pervasive French culture assimilates and absorbs their Arab heritage.[29]

Benguigui's 2008 documentary, *9–3, Mémoire d'un territoire* (*9–3, Memory of a Territory*), broadcast on Canal +, refers to the number (93)

27. See Portuges, *Le colonial féminin.*

28. Maryse Fauvel, "Yamina Benguigui's *Inch'Allah dimanche:* Unveiling Hybrid Identities," *Studies in French Cinema* 4/2 (2004): 147–56.

29. Benguigui (Chevalier de la Légion d'Honneur des arts et des lettres; Ordre national du Mèrite), in addition to being a distinguished filmmaker accomplished across genres, is also an adviser to the French government on immigration. See Mouna Isddine, "Yamina pionnière du beur," *Maroc Hebdo International* 763 (19–25 October 2007): 51.

that was given to the *département* of Constantine, in what was then French Algeria, before that number was used to designate Seine-Saint-Denis, the Parisian *banlieue* where Spanish, Portuguese, and Maghrebi familes lived and worked until the 1960s when its populations became ghettoized according to racial and ethnic origin. The film covers the history of the '9–3' from 1850 to 2005, with some fifty interviews of inhabitants recorded in their homes. What primarily interests Benguigui here is the words, the emotional human testimonies recorded by a microphone equally available to every witness; thus the viewer eventually understands how the "9–3" became a theater of urban violence in 2005, and why many of its people remain viscerally attached to their country of origin.

This rich tapestry of intercultural, self-reflexive cinematic narratives crosses boundaries of place and genre, and summarizes a number of diverse and contradictory impulses: the desire to belong and to break away; an urge to reject the other and a concomitant wish to accept otherness as a part of the self; a longing for harmony among faiths and cultures together with the need to assert the self within the collectivity. It is striking that to note that the majority of films under discussion are first features, perhaps suggesting the attractiveness and viability of this format for filmmakers committed to inscribing their own and others' experience of immigration, border crossing and hybrid identities, whether in semi-autobiographical or fictional form. Deploying a range of visual strategies and narrative structures, they contest repressive political and social practices, often within a triadic narrative configuration that foregrounds sisters, friends, and other women, gesturing toward the construction of a collective happiness. Observing and documenting the eruptions of aggression in which friends and neighbors may become enemies, they also testify to the achievements made possible by women artists performing the transnational as a cinematic space of exchange and collaboration.

## II. Representing Space in Cinema: City, Suburb, and Countryside

## LUDOVIC CORTADE

# The Spatial Evacuation of Politics: Landscape, Power, and the "Monarch" in Robert Guédiguian's *The Last Mitterand*

Since the 1980s, French cinema has been characterized by the success of films with a strong national heritage component that corresponds to the French collective imaginary. Landscape appears among the privileged vectors of identity in contemporary French cinema, in the guise of *essentialization* and *absorption.* The essentialization of landscape consists in associating it with the traditional attributes of regional identity or "Frenchness." Such is the case in the Provence of *Jean de Florette* and *Manon des Sources/Manon of the Source,* based on Marcel Pagnol's novels (Claude Berri, 1986); in the portrayal of Paris in *Le fabuleux destin d'Amélie Poulain/Amélie Poulain* (Jean-Pierre Jeunet, 2001) that revives the image of urban sociability before the war; or in the Auvergne countryside of *Être et avoir/To Be and To Have* (Nicolas Philibert, 2002) that celebrates an educational utopia in a bucolic setting of an "eternal France" spared the trials and tribulations of the city. Landscape, then, is an intangible component of French identity corresponding to a genre: the film of heritage and nostalgia.[1] The essentialized landscape, focusing on identity, corresponds to what André Gardies calls the "landscape-background," which "contributes to the referential anchoring of the diegetic world. For this, it is very often organized so as to be recognized by the viewer by privileging expected components."[2] By reinforcing the collective imaginary, the representation of the "landscape-background" in contemporary French cinema responds to the challenges regarding identity that are tied to globaliza-

---

1. Phil Powrie, *French Cinema in the 1980s—Nostalgia and the Crisis of Masculinity* (Oxford: Oxford University Press), 13–27; Powrie, *French Cinema in the 1990s—Continuity and Difference* (Oxford: Oxford University Press), 1–10.

2. André Gardies, "Le paysage comme moment narratif" in Jean Mottet, ed., *Les paysages du cinéma* (Seyssel: Champ Vallon, 1999), 145.

**YFS 115,** *New Spaces for French and Francophone Cinema,* ed. James F. Austin, © 2009 by Yale University.

tion and the "social disconnect" of which the "young French cinema" of the 1990s is symptomatic.[3] The identity function of landscape's essentialization is reinforced by the frequency of the absorption motif whereby characters forge a matricial link to space by cloistering themselves in enclosed and reassuring spaces, in both heritage cinema and the cinema of the "look." In heritage cinema, the landscaped retreats of Sainte Colombe in *Tous les matins du monde/All the Mornings of the World* (Corneau, 1991) exemplify absorption. The so-called cinema of the "look," an expression that refers to a certain postmodern French cinema of the 1980s, is also distinguished by the body's absorption in a landscape, whether urban or rural. Protective spaces dominate: for example, the feeling of isolation produced by the matricial link uniting characters to apartments seemingly without windows in *Diva* (Beineix, 1981); the subterranean life in the bowels of the Parisian subway in *Subway* (Besson, 1985); the total submersion of the swimmer's body in the sea until death in *Le grand bleu/The Big Blue* (Besson, 1988); or Yves Montand's mystic quest through the forest in *IP5—L'île aux pachydermes/IP5: The Island of Pachyderms* (Beineix, 1992). One hypothesis worth exploring posits that this portrayal of body and landscape is a relic of the figure of absorption, as Michael Fried has pointed out for eighteenth and nineteenth century French painting.[4] Within the limits of this article, it is, however, from a political point of view that I would like to broach the question of landscape's essentialization and the body's absorption therein. One possible interpretation of this question would be that heritage cinema and the cinema of the "look," by respectively favoring a nostalgic "patrimonialization" of French history and an "advertising" aesthetic, contribute to a lack of political consciousness.[5] Indeed, essentialization and absorption raise the question of landscape's ideological function in cinema. We need to analyze the role played by the "landscape-background" in the constitution of a national ideology (the myth of "eternal France") that aims to de-politicize the cinema.

3. Francis Vanoye, in Michel Marie, ed. *Le jeune cinéma français* (Paris: Nathan, 1998), 56.

4. Michael Fried, *Absorption and Theatricality: Painting and Beholder in the Age of Diderot* (Berkeley: University of California Press, 1980), and *Courbet's Realism* (Chicago: University of Chicago Press, 1990).

5. See in particular: Marie-Thérèse Journot, *Le courant de "l'esthétique publicitaire" dans le cinéma français des années 80. La modernité en crise: Beineix, Besson, Carax* (Paris: L'Harmattan, 2004).

In their article "Cinéma/Idéologie/Critique," published in 1969, Jean Narboni and Jean-Louis Comolli examine the different relationships that the cinema maintains with ideology, and they establish a typology. The critics distinguish four categories of films: those that are entirely forged by ideology, in form and in content; those that, conversely, critique ideology on the level of form and content; those that, despite an overtly political intention, adopt a traditional form, thus compromising the whole of the critical approach; and finally, in a last category, Narboni and Comolli expose the ambivalence of certain films that, though forged by the dominant ideology on the level of content, manage nevertheless to criticize this ideology through their style.[6] A subsequent article (1970), written collectively by the Cahiers du cinéma's editorial staff and devoted to John Ford's film Young Mister Lincoln, emphasizes the relationship that landscape maintains with ideology: it is in leaning against a tree, along a river bank, that Abraham Lincoln discovers capitalism's "natural" character.[7] For the article's authors, capitalism is presented as an intangible given, since "the acquisition and the defense of property are presented here as a matter of the natural, indeed of the divine," which is reinforced by an aesthetic of "transparence" where the landscape is an important element. According to the Cahiers du cinéma, Ford manages nonetheless to distance himself in relation to ideology, thanks to an internal critique based on style, allowing Ford to be put in Comolli and Narboni's fourth category.

In this article, I would like to analyze the portrayal of landscape and politics in Robert Guédiguian's Le promeneur du Champs de Mars/ The Last Mitterrand (2005), which is devoted to the final months of François Mitterrand's life and is based on conversations that the president had with Georges-Marc Benamou in the months before his death in 1996.[8] The film raises the following questions: What is landscape's function in the construction of a national imaginary and does the director have a critical approach toward landscape's ideological function?

6. Cahiers du Cinéma 216 (October 1969): 13–14. Translated into English as "Cinema/Ideology/Criticism," in Cahiers du Cinema 1969–1972; The Politics of Representation, ed. Nick Brown (London: BFI, 1985).

7. "Young Mister Lincoln de John Ford" (collective article), Cahiers du cinéma 223 (August 1970): 29–47. Translated into English in Screen 13 (1972).

8. The film's French title, "Le promeneur du Champ de Mars" [The Walker on the Champ de Mars] refers to Mitterrand's last place of residence in Paris on the Avenue Frédéric le Play. See Georges-Marc Benamou, Le dernier Mitterrand (Paris: Plon, 1996).

In other words, should we consider landscape's portrayal in Guédiguian's film as a validation of the ideology of "eternal France" evacuating politics, or rather, on the contrary, as a critique of the de-politicization of Mitterrandian France?

The film is characterized by a de-politicization that depends first of all on a relationship with time, one based on amnesia and nostalgia. The film is remarkable for its absence of reflection on the Collaboration during World War II, as well as its resigned acknowledgment of the lack of left-wing alternatives openly hostile to French free-market capitalism in the 1990s. The unclear aspects of Mitterrand's past in the Vichy government are not really seen as problematic: despite the journalist's probing questions, these aspects of Mitterrand's past appear like a historical accident or a youthful error in the life of someone who had not yet received presidential consecration. A woman who was in the French Resistance and who knew the future president during the war seems to want to protect him: "The truth, and nothing but the truth? That's what you hope for? I find you rather presumptuous. . . . Let him manage with his memory. You know, memory is something very personal. The only judge in this matter is him and him alone." As for the young librarian from the Vichy archives, she shows herself capable of compassion when confronted with what seems to her like the relentlessness of memory: "Leave him in peace; he's old and is going to die. I don't like this guy, but well . . . I hate vultures." Politics is furthermore reduced to an acknowledgment of powerlessness, tinted with nostalgia. The discussions between the journalist and the journalist's father-in-law, a Communist activist, are without a political dimension and, moreover, reveal the despondency of the working class caught between pessimism and a nostalgia for the time when the Communist party played an influential role in French political life, before its neutralization by the Socialists. In *The Last Mitterrand*, de-politicization occurs not only in the relation to time, but also in the work of space. I wish to show here that the portrayal of landscape in *The Last Mitterrand* is essentialized, dissolving all problematization of contemporary politics to leave room for the melancholic reappearance of a monarchical conception of power, which is the refuge of the national imaginary as it is confronted with what Guédiguian calls "the end of the Socialist idea."[9]

9. Robert Guédiguian, *Ibid.*, 30.

# FROM POETIC HORIZON TO PRESIDENTIAL CARTOGRAPHY

The first appearance of François Mitterrand, played by Michel Bouquet, occurs aboard a helicopter flying over Beauce in the company of Antoine, a young left-wing journalist. Although this episode is fictitious (there is no mention of it in the book of interviews), Guédiguian and his two scriptwriters use it at the very beginning of the film. Several high-angle shots overlook grain fields,[10] while the illustrious passenger begins a lecture on literary geography: "Antoine, look at that. You must reread all of Péguy. 'Two thousand years of labor have made of this earth an endless reservoir for the new ages.'" The president pursues the quotation: "'Thus we sail toward our cathedral. A rosary of millstones floats here and there.' I discovered this poem by Péguy in high school. 'A rosary of millstones.' . . . How better to express the mystical taking root? To undertake everything so that mysticism is not devoured by the politics to which it gave birth. That is what we call an ideal; it sums up the character." The quotations are excerpts from the poem "Présentation de la Beauce à Notre Dame de Chartres" appearing in *La tapisserie de Notre-Dame,* a text that Charles Péguy wrote after a three-day pilgrimage in June 1912 to show his gratitude to the Virgin for the recovery of one of his sick sons.[11] These quotations, chosen by the film's illustrious individual, reveal that the relationship to landscape is based on absorption and essentialization.

Absorption depends on the theme of the "mystical taking root," that is, on the access of the body to an entity that transcends it: eternal France. It is also articulated in the definition of a literary space with which the reader merges, thanks to aesthetics. This is an aesthetization [*artialisation*] of landscape that is only perceived through a corpus of literary and artistic works. As Oscar Wilde observed: "Life imitates art far more than art imitates life. . . At present, people see fogs, not because there are fogs, but because poets and painters have taught them

10. The grain fields here refer to Beauce, a fertile area encompassing about 600,000 hectares, devoted to agriculture. Located southwest of Paris, it is considered the grain belt of France. Its principal city is Chartres. [Translator's note]

11. Charles Péguy, "Présentation de la Beauce à Notre Dame de Chartres,"*Œuvres poétiques complètes* (Paris: Gallimard, Bibliothèque de la Pléiade, 1957, republished 1975), 896–907. This poem appears to have been translated into English for a sound recording, not available to this translator. See Charles Péguy, "Presentation of the Beauce region to Notre Dame of Chartres," in *20th Century French Poetry* [sound recording], Paul A. Mankin, narrator (Smithsonian Folkways Records, 1965).

the mysterious loveliness of such effects."[12] In this sequence, landscape is perceived through a geographical imaginary filled with literature: the grain field is not only a physical reality, in the geographical sense of the term, it is also a literary invention. The beauty of the Beauce landscape surrounding the Chartres cathedral is only visible to the president because Péguy sings its praises.[13] As for landscape's essentialization, it is worked out on the basis of the values of labor, fertility, and abundance that inscribe the body in an entity gifted with two bodies, one both immaterial and rooted in a landscape. The sequence of "mystical taking root" thus depends on the passage "from an aesthetic landscape to an ideological landscape" that is instigated by the presidential figure.[14]

Using the arguments in Comolli and Narboni's text "Cinema/Ideologie/Critique" and those in the collective article devoted to Ford's *Young Mister Lincoln*, it is possible to put forward the following hypothesis: Guédiguian adopts landscape's role in the construction of the national ideology in order to better examine this latter stylistically. In this sequence, the ideology of power and the nation appears in the gap between the verticality of the film's mise-en-scène and the horizontality that characterizes Péguy's poetic oeuvre. If Guédiguian uses a series of high angle shots taken on board the helicopter, it is because it corresponds to a cartographic "eye-world" whose meaning is above all political: from this point of view, verticality is a panoptism.[15] However,

12. Oscar Wilde, *The Decay of Lying*, preface by Hugh Haughton (London; New York: Syrens, 1995); citation originally taken from Alain Roger's *Court traité du paysage* (Paris: Gallimard, 1997).

13. It is worth noting that even the name "Beauce" is potentially an artistic wellspring, depending on the breadth of reading of the one encountering the toponym: will the reader retain the scholarly etymology (the word comes in fact from the Latinized Celtic "belsa," a cultivated plain designating a field), or Rabelais' legendary story? Rabelais "invented" the word by rescuing the name of the famous plain from oblivion; it was then only a forest in the episode of the attack of the hornets on Gargantua's mare. The horse responded by moving its tail so brusquely that it cleared the woods all around: "She knocked down woods as a reaper does grass, so that since then there have been neither woods nor hornets, but the whole region was reduced to open country. Seeing which Gargantua took great pleasure without otherwise boasting of it, and said to his men: 'I think this is beautiful [Je trouve beau ce],' whence this region has since been called la Beauce." François Rabelais, *Gargantua*, chapt. XVI, in *The Complete Works of François Rabelais*, trans. Donald M. Frame (University of California Press: 1998), 41.

14. François Walter, *Les figures paysagères de la nation—territoire et paysage en Europe (XVIe–XXe siécle)* (Paris: Éditions de l'École des hautes études en sciences sociales, 2004), 147.

15. Christine Buci-Glucksmann, *L'oeil cartographique de l'art* (Paris: Galilée, 1996),

Péguy's relationship to landscape is different: in the "Présentation de la Beauce à Notre Dame de Chartres," the succession of toponyms and the semantic field of the text mark off a real geographical journey leading the poet to evoke "the long path we follow in Beauce" (906). From the storefront of the *Cahiers de la Quinzaine*[16] to the cathedral, the perception is definitely that of a body crisscrossing the landscape. Péguy challenges the map's vertical panoptism to embrace "the immense horizon" (901) that is revealed over the course of the journey (he evokes the "beveled road," the "hill," the "crossroads," the "slopes," and the "high terrace"). As Jean-Marc Besse observes, Péguy is not attempting to find "a high vantage point in order to encompass with a glance, thanks to the distance of the point of view and to the open view that distance allows, all aspects of a region."[17] This is why "there is no overhang, no inclusive synthesis, only towns that are gone through, orientation problems with departures and arrivals, directions to follow."[18] The substitution of cinematographic verticality for poetic horizontality shows the extent of the process of landscape's domestication by the person who incarnates a unifying national conscience: the presidential flight freezes Beauce in a way that ties a political and national heritage value to it. The "mystical taking root" is a shedding of a physical body acceding to the *corpus mysticum* of the monarch. As Guédiguian emphasizes, the film deals "with the death of a king" (Michel Bouquet defines his character as "a very great monarch").[19] If there exists such a close bond between the king and the landscape, it is because they both have two bodies: just as the king possesses a physical body and a mystical body guaranteeing the continuity of his power over time, so the landscape is both a simple grain field flown over on a winter morning and the essence of "eternal France."

---

11–48; Yves Lacoste, *La géographie, ça sert, d'abord, à faire la guerre* (Paris: Maspéro, 1976).

16. The *Cahiers de la Quinzaine* was a literary magazine to which Péguy was the main contributor and editor. [Translator's note].

17. Jean-Marc Besse, "Dans les plis du monde. Paysage et philosophie selon Péguy" in *Voir la terre. Six essais sur le paysage et la géographie* (Arles: Actes Sud, 2000), 157.

18. *Ibid.*, 154–155.

19. According to Guédiguian, the film retraces "the death of a king." Cited in Alan Riding, "Socialist Monarch, Portrayed as a Man," *New York Times*, March 5, 2005. See also Michel Bouquet's interview with Eric Moulin in *Les promeneurs. Mitterrand & Bouquet—"Le Promeneur du Champ de Mars," un film de Robert Guédiguian* (Paris: Editions de l'œil, 2007), 35.

## THE LANDSCAPE IS A PORTRAIT OF THE KING

The cartographic point of view over the landscape and the king's portrait have this in common: they are both supported by the dogma of transubstantiation. As Louis Marin demonstrates, corroborating Antoine Arnault and Pierre Nicole's *Logique de Port-Royal,* a portrait of the king and a map imply the idea of a real presence: "And in this way, one says straightaway and without fuss that a portrait of Caesar is Caesar and a map of Italy is Italy."[20] We then understand that the transitory and uncertain length of a walk, such as it appears in fact in Péguy, was hardly compatible with the cinematographic portrayal of power that has a duty to reveal "a permanent and infinite quality of the king."[21] Such is the function of the high-angle shots from the helicopter that flies over the landscape in which the legitimacy of presidential power takes shape, following the example of the king who "states the length, space, and the essence of the country."[22] The president, favoring the motif of mystical absorption, becomes in this way a "man-landscape," while inversely, "France is a person": the monarch-president.[23] We can, however, wonder about the ability of the discrepancy between Péguy's poetry and Guédiguian's stylistic treatment to provoke a critique of a politics that would be a mysticism of rootedness. In other words, can we propose, returning to Comolli and Narboni's analytical framework, that the high-angle shots form an internal critique of the ideology of which the film seems to be the product? It seems doubtful: the left-wing journalist is enthusiastic about the president's culture, and the "landscape-background" becomes a popular cliché, an Epinal print[24] that gives the viewer the feeling of a national identity of landscape. When the film was released, the filmmaker himself acknowledged having sought "the image that one often has of the French landscape," thereby acknowledging that a film about power had a duty to satisfy the geographical imaginary of the public. He thus registers

20. Quotation from *La logique de Port-Royal* (204–205), cited in Louis Marin, "Les voies de la carte," in (coll.) *Cartes et figures de la terre* (Paris: Centre Georges Pompidou, 1980), 47.

21. *Ibid.*, 167.

22. Alain Boureau, "Le Roi," in Pierre Nora, *Les lieux de mémoire* 3 (Paris: Gallimard, 1992), 789.

23. Alain Tapié and Jeanette Zwingenberger, *L'homme-paysage* (Paris and Lille: Somogy and the Palais des Beaux-Arts de Lille, 2006); Jules Michelet, *Tableau de la France,* *Œuvres complètes* 4 (Paris: Flammarion, 1974), 383.

24. Epinal: the author here makes reference to the fact that the town of Epinal is known for producing popular and pious imagery. [Translator's note]

the question of identity in what could be called the viewers' *horizon of landscape expectation*, giving them the feeling of territoriality: "I was very eager to do a 'little tour of France.'"[25]

The conjunction of affectivity, absorption, and essentialization allows us to understand why the president admires in Péguy the fact that "mysticism is not consumed by the politics to which it gave birth." It is thus not surprising that the director's editing juxtaposes the episode of the flight over Beauce with a visit to the basilica of Saint-Denis, necropolis of French kings. Accompanied by the journalist, François Mitterrand admires the recumbent statues of François I and Claude of France: "Run your hand over the stone; it isn't cold. It is drenched in sweat." A close-up shows the president's face and his black-gloved hand in contact with the mortuary statues that seem to writhe with pain in the smooth, white stone. In this shot, Guédiguian shows the president's constitutive bi-corporality, the one that imitates Christ in possessing two natures: human and divine.[26] When Mitterand leaves the basilica, he admits being conscious of the survival of medieval political theology in the history of the Fifth Repubublic, while also delivering a bitter acknowledgment of the evolution of power: "You know, Antoine, and I say this without any presumptuousness, I am the last of the great presidents. In short, I mean the last in the line of de Gaulle. After me, there will be no others in France. Because of Europe and globalization, nothing will be the same."

The president's reflection takes account of the relative desacralization of power that results from its tendency toward a growing humanization, leading to a "disillusionment of the world." This desacralization is explained in the film by the weakening of the nation-states' decision-making ability, the inter-dependence and the spreading of economic exchange on an international scale (recent studies also point to the role of the media's omnipresence and of a president's use of a "politics of compassion").[27] This evolution appears in the film as an unenviable outcome that conflicts with the left-wing journalist's fascina-

25. Guédiguian, "L'intérêt, c'était d'allégoriser Mitterand" [Interview with Françoise Audé et Yann Tobin], *Positif* 528 (February 2005): 31.

26. Ernst Kantorowicz, *The King's Two Bodies; a Study in Mediaeval Political Theology* (Princeton, N.J.: Princeton University Press, 1957). George-Marc Benamou, *op. cit.*, 54–55.

27. Marcel Gauchet, *Le désenchantement du monde* (Paris: Gallimard, 1985); Olivier Mongin et Georges Vigarello, *Sarkozy. Corps et âme d'un président* (Paris: Perrin 2008).

tion with the president's ability to unite the nation. The tone is not that of political critique, but of nostalgia for the presidential aura: "What he had just shown me was the final stage, the petrification. The president's body had become the body of us all: a national body." The final stage is not death, but the process by which the president's physical body is coupled with a mystical body in which history and its dialectic movement are abolished. Moreover, the scene where the president has his bath at the Elysée and appears naked before the left-wing journalist demeans the aura of the monarch's dual nature: if Antoine is uneasy at the sight of the president's physical body, it is because his conception of power is based on a nostalgia for the *corpus mysticum*.

## THE TREE: A SYNCRETISM
## OF NATIONAL IDEOLOGIES

The evacuation of politics is a neutralization of the dialectical movement of history; thus the care with which the filmmaker bases the film on a circular structure, and this through the landscape component that establishes a parallel between the first sequence representing the president, and the final shot of the film: *The Last Mitterrand* begins with the flight over Beauce and concludes with a shot depicting a tree. The last sequence shows the President at death's door: after having seen Antoine one last time, he asks to be left alone in his room. The film then ends with a vertical pan that tilts upward, showing a pine tree in a low-angle shot. The choice of the type of tree may appear surprising when one knows that the presidential emblem created in 1981 depicts the oak and the olive tree, two trees that evoke strength and peace respectively, and the relations between the developed countries of the North and those of the South. Nevertheless, the pine here refers to the property of Latché, in the Landes, where the president resided in the days before his death in Paris in January 1996. The tree's meaning is ambivalent, much like the president's ideological complexity, in which socialist ideas often coincided with the resurgence of a provincial, conservative education. The importance of landscape is noticeable in the background of the official poster of Mitterrand's 1981 campaign election, accompanied by the famous slogan "Tranquil strength": socialism as the image of a political man united with a rural, reassuring landscape, presenting in this way a guarantee of stability, indeed of tradition. The last shot of the film offers a unifying symbol in this regard: it puts an end to the dialectic opposing right and left by symbolically reuniting them. In *The Last Mitterrand*, the tree concludes the film while also marking the end of history.

On the one hand, the pine can be interpreted as a symbol of the Republic, alluding to the famous "trees of liberty," whose meaning and revolutionary function were established by Abbé Grégoire in 1794.[28] The symbolic system of these "left-wing" trees would endure throughout the nineteenth century, as is shown by Victor Hugo's lines written for the planting of a tree of liberty during the celebration of the Second Republic in 1848. It is also evident in Hugo's poem entitled "In Planting the Acorn of the Oak Tree of the United States of Europe in the Garden of the Hauteville House, July 14, 1870." The date of the title is the actual date on which the poet planted the tree in his garden on Guernsey, after which he returned to France, following the declaration of the Third Republic.[29] On the other hand, the tree can just as well be interpreted as a symbol of the right, illustrated by the episode of the walk in the seventh chapter of Maurice Barrès' *Les déracinés*.[30]

In Guédiguian's film, the tree goes beyond the nation's political divisions. It appears as an element of the integration of an identity on the basis of a unifying and affective relationship with the landscape. At the level of the anthropology of power, this pine is a relic of the *Ancien Régime:* like the king, the tree is the identity vector uniting subjects in a common body. Similarly endowed with two bodies, it links together the visible and the invisible world: "It simultaneously offers the figure of a natural, organic body, open to transcendence, and it displays a permanence over time."[31] The tree is not only a living organism doomed

28. The Convention had at that time entrusted, by decree, the planting and the upkeep of the liberty trees "to the care of good citizens, so that in each town the tree of liberty flowers under the aegis of French liberty." Abbé Grégoire, quoted in Robert Dumas, "L'arbre, symbole politique ambivalent," *Le débat* 142 (Paris: Gallimard, 2006), 177.

29. "A tree is a beautiful and true symbol of freedom! Freedom has its roots in the people's heart; it raises and spreads out its branches in the sky; like a tree, it continuously grows and covers generations with its shadow," from "Planting of the Liberty Tree, Place des Vosges" (Speech from March 2, 1848) in Victor Hugo, *Œuvres complétes—Politique* (Paris: Robert Laffont, 1985), 147. "Let us sow the acorn, and may it be an immense oak tree! / Let us sow law, and may it be just, glorious and clear / Let us sow man and may he be the people! / Let us sow France / And may she be Humanity," excerpt from the poem "In Planting the Acorn of the Oak Tree of the United States of Europe in the Garden of the *Hauteville House* July 14, 1870," *Les quatre vents de l'esprit*, in Victor Hugo, *Œuvres complètes—Poésie III* (Paris: Robert Laffont, 1985), 1373.

30. The chapter relates the stroll of Taine who evokes the pleasure that the sight of a tree he is fond of gives him; Maurice Barrès, *Les déracinés* (Paris: Laffont, 1994), 596–98, quoted in Dumas, *op. cit.*, 179.

31. *Ibid.*, 172.

to decline since it is also endowed with an ontology: it is the essence of power and justice. The genealogical tree maintains the continuity of a familial or royal line over time; it ensures the link between generations: "this order of filiation that the plantlike body of the tree embodies implies a logic of incorporation. It is as if, by analogy, families become the leaves and branches of a same tree, the cells of a same body, the political body incarnated by the king's sacred body, which produces the monarchy beyond his death by generating his successor."[32] The tree also symbolizes the essence of justice: the vision of a young Abraham Lincoln discovering law as he leans against a tree in Ford's film, just as the last shot of Guédiguian's film may be interpreted as the relic of popular imagery depicting Saint Louis dispensing justice under an oak tree.[33]

By the tree's ambivalence, *The Last Mitterrand* evacuates the dialectic of the political game in favor of the incorporation and the absorption of the presidential body in an essentialized landscape. In *The Last Mitterrand*, the depoliticization of French history appears in all its fullness only because it is inscribed in an ageless space. It is responsible for a national conscience unified by a relic of medieval theology of monarchical power. Of course, Guédiguian emphasizes the contradictions of socialist power and the disappointments that it causes left-wing activists when the reformist fervor clashes with economic realities and the personalization of a president turned monarch. Nonetheless, the film is more an acknowledgment of powerlessness than a critique of an ideology of national identity. In the film, the nostalgia for identity under the cover of an essentialized landscape is not problematic for the left-wing journalist who takes down the President's words, as if a withdrawal into national identity was always preferable to the difficulties of globalization. The question of the anchoring of identity is moreover a definite characteristic of the director's recent films: in his 1997 film, *Marius et Jeannette/Marius and Jeannette*, Guédiguian favored a "warm tale" in regionalist and nostalgic accents over a genuine social critique.[34] In *The Last Mitterrand*, the weakness of the critique of national ideology makes the film seem like the product of a cinema in search of territoriality. It is thus hardly surprising

32. *Ibid.*, 171.

33. The author makes reference here to an emblematic image of King Louis IX that is frequently reproduced in children's history books. [Translator's Note]

34. On this point, see: Steven Ungar, "*Marius et Jeannette:* A Political Tale," *IRIS* 29 (Spring 2000): 39–52.

that the film gives the impression, not of a critique of the false hopes created by French socialism from 1981 to 1995, but of a time when the search for spatial identity appears to be the only alternative to the crisis of socialism.

If, following Comolli and Narboni's article, the *Cahiers du cinéma*'s editorial staff analyzed the originality of *Young Mister Lincoln* by showing that Ford managed in his film to criticize the ideology of which he himself was the product, it is worth noting that thirty-five years later, this same journal sees in *The Last Mitterrand* a total evacuation of politics: "Here we are: begun under the accumulated auspices of Péguy, the Chartres cathedral, and the recumbent statues of the kings it shelters, this films speaks of eternal France. Basically, if Mitterrand has no difficulty playing on his charm as well as on what is invisible . . . it is because he really expects that in his person the two merge, producing a sacred body. . . . In the miracle of this immaculate transmission, notice is given to that basely material thing called politics."[35]

—Translated by Sally Shafto

---

35. François Bégaudeau, in *Cahiers du cinema* 598 (February 2005): 28.

JAMES F. AUSTIN

# Destroying the *banlieue:* Reconfigurations of Suburban Space in French Film

Violence struck the French *banlieue* (suburbs) in October and November of 2005, over the course of three weeks, and then again in November of 2007, beginning outside Paris and spreading spectacularly throughout a France in which several buildings and hundreds of automobiles—sometimes over a thousand—burned each night. The situation recalled similar incidents decades earlier, in 1981 and 1990 in the suburbs of Lyon. Most of the violence was not only predictable but predicted by a *banlieue* cinema that had, in the face of worsening conditions in the suburb, sounded multiple warning sirens.

*La haine (Hate)* (Kassovitz, 1995) remains the best-heard of these cinematic warnings; widely noted for its unflinching representations and its artistic qualities, it became a highly influential portrayal of the problems of the French *banlieue.* As *La haine* has been very thoroughly explored in criticism, and rightly so, I will merely recall the film's framing allegory and memorable refrain, which speaks to the precariousness of existence felt in the suburbs: "It's the story of man who falls from a fifty-storey building. During his fall, the guy keeps telling himself, 'So far so good, so far so good, so far so good,' but the important thing isn't the fall, it's the landing."[1] These words also serve as an apt observation about the state of much of the *banlieue* cinema itself, more likely to show the fall (the brutality, discrimination, poverty, drugs, and blight), rather than the shock of the landing, that is, the riots.

Drawing on Carrie Tarr's definition of *banlieue* filmmaking, I will examine movies that represent the life and space of the *banlieue,* the rundown, multi-ethnic, working-class or poor housing projects located

---

1. All translations are my own, except where indicated.

**YFS 115,** *New Spaces for French and Francophone Cinema,* ed. James F. Austin,
© 2009 by Yale University.

outside of major French cities.[2] Most *banlieue* films feature restive youths who struggle with themselves, their families, or repressive police officers in an often violent, dystopic, ex-centric suburban space dominated by concrete, their existence punctuated at best by brief moments of community, hope, or aesthetic promise. Representations of the *banlieue* often emphasize features common to dystopias, such as an oppressive state or signs of a failed Utopia, in this case the ubiquitous greyness of the *barres,* the large mid-rise apartment buildings that came to define the cheaply-built "temporary" suburban housing projects from the 1960s, and that are a degraded version of the Utopian aspirations of Le Corbusier's *Ville radieuse* (radiant city).

To understand the space of the suburb, it is important to recall that in contrast to Paris, which fixed its *de facto* city limits in 1845, and then its official boundaries in 1860, the suburbs around Paris have known no such limit, and indeed, the space of the *banlieue* itself has grown immensely over the last one hundred and fifty years. As a crucial vector of the French imaginary responsive to a broad public, the cinema can tell us much about this underexplored spatial other of the more celebrated Paris, what desires concerning the *banlieue* lurk under the surface, and which (radical) ones are welling up into the social imaginary. These include political revolution and sedition, or simply the desire to eliminate physically the space of the *banlieue* altogether, that is, to destroy the *banlieue.*

## SPATIAL DESTRUCTION

While the severity of the various troubles described in the *banlieue* cinema and experienced in the suburbs certainly increased with time, in nature they remained static. Indeed, from Mehdi Charef's *Le thé au harem (Tea in the Harem)* in 1985, to Kassovitz's *La haine* ten years later, to Ameur-Zaïmeche's *Wesh wesh, qu'est-ce qui se passe?* (Wesh wesh, What's Up?, 2001), the *banlieue* cinema appears as immobile in nature as the state response to the *banlieues* themselves,[3] though there

2. Carrie Tarr, *Reframing Difference: Beur and Banlieue Filmmaking in France* (Manchester: Manchester University Press, 2005), 2–3. Compared to the "immigrant film," "*banlieue*" film is less focused on issues of cultural difference, integration, etc., and more on the *banlieue* and life in it.

3. The latest in a series of *plan banlieue*—in which the French state typically promises less unemployment, better education, public transportation, and social services funding—though announced in February 2008, already shows signs of being scaled back.

are significant exceptions. The latter feature a distinct urban and sub-urban imaginary that can be explored both for diagnoses of the essential problem of the *banlieue,* and for radical proposals of a cure. Such is the case for *Ma 6-t va crack-er* (My C-T is Gonna Crack) (Richet, 1997), *Jeunesse dorée* (Golden Youth) (Ghorab-Volta, 2002), and *Les triplettes de belleville* (*The Triplets of Belleville*) (Chomet, 2003). While *Les triplettes* is clearly not a *banlieue* film, my intent is not only to outline the conventions of a specific genre, but also to look to a broader French film culture and its imagination of the *banlieue* and urban space. I will delineate, then, both the political and economic causes cited in the films, and the "solutions" that the films present, which are: 1) violent political revolution; 2) a physical destruction of the built suburb; 3) the assimilation or integration of suburban space into urban space.

It would seem at first that the problem of the French *banlieue* is necessarily one of space: by definition, the suburbs are outside the city proper, and the economic and social problems associated with these places seem endemic to their location on that "circular purgatory" looking in at the urban "paradise" (often Paris) at the center.[4] It is "out there" that the cars burn, that the riots recur, that police stations, schools, and libraries are destroyed and degraded. But as the influential theoretician of space Henri Lefebvre pointed out, space does not just happen, rather it is generated, as each society, state, or economic system, produces its own social space:

> every society—and hence every mode of production with its subvari-ants (i.e. all those societies which exemplify the general concept) pro-duces a space, its own space. . . . Each society offers up its own peculiar space, as it were, as an "object" for analysis and overall theoretical ex-plication. I say each society, but it would be more accurate to say each mode of production, along with its specific relations of production.[5]

The *banlieue* is not, in this light, a spatial accident or fatality, but is rather generated as a spatial function of some larger system. Lefebvre emphasizes the role of the state in supporting the capitalist system in producing, through violence and political power, a separate, dominated space of repression and constraint; worrisome groups (the "dangerous

4. See François Maspero's oft-cited *Les passagers du Roissy-Express* (Paris: Seuil, 1990), 24.
5. Henri Lefebvre, *The Production of Space,* trans. Donald Nicholson-Smith (Oxford: Blackwell Publishing, 1991). All citations in this article are from the English edition.

classes"), e.g. workers, are pushed to the periphery, while the center becomes a rarefied concentration of wealth, political power, and decision making (Lefebvre, *The Production of Space*, 358, 375).

The film *Ma 6-t va crack-er* seeks to redefine this spatial, political, and economic configuration, described by Lefebvre and so persistent in France, while exploring its underlying causes. Throughout this extremely talkative film, the young men of the suburban housing project, who are mostly of North African origin, are eminently conscious of their status and the resulting lack of economic opportunity, noting that unemployment is so extreme that they see little prospect for their future. In this, they mirror the experience of France itself, in which suburban residents are excluded from economic opportunity, and where second- and third-generation immigrants, especially those of North African Arab or Black Sub-Saharan origin, suffer chronic societal and racial discrimination. As for solutions, the end of the film proposes a striking one: when the police arrive at the site of a very damaged car in the *cité* (projects), and when they shoot and kill a young (armed) man, streams of other young men quickly fill the space and destroy entire rows of cars, bashing and burning them, along with a public telephone. Riot police mass on the outskirts of the scene, and the ensuing nighttime battle scene, filmed to the inflammatory lyrics of the rap song "Sédition," is illuminated by the Molotov cocktails thrown at the police, who are engulfed in flames. Indeed, this "solution" is one in which both cars and people burn.

*Ma 6-t* is careful to show us the destruction of that public telephone along with the automobiles. By destroying cars and telephones, technologies of communication and mobility (of people, of voice), produced by icons of French industry and capitalism such as Renault and Peugeot or France Télécom, the characters are (seditiously) cutting themselves off from the *polis* and its economic order, constituting a separate space. And unlike in so many other *banlieue* movies that prominently feature a trip to Paris, these young men remain firmly at home, making of their "occupied territory"—as they ruefully refer to it—a place where police fear to tread.

In light of this film, the actions of October–November 2005 (and of November 2007) begin to make more sense. The real destruction of the cars in the suburbs can be read as a mostly unconscious desire of the young men to fight against the political and economic system that generated the vehicles, with the additional irony that it was the automobile industry that originally employed and lured to France in the 1950s,

1960s, and 1970s the immigrant parents of those who now, unemployed, destroy the cars. It is also the destruction of a symbol of the lack of adequate public transportation in the isolated suburb, and an act of financial aggression against those relatively more prosperous inhabitants of the suburbs who can afford a vehicle.

At the very end of *Ma 6-t*, after the violence, a quotation of article 35 of the Declaration of the Rights of Man and of the Citizen appears on the screen: "When the government violates the rights of the people, insurrection is for the people and for each portion of the people the most sacred of rights and the most indispensable of duties."[6] It would be difficult to be clearer in this film about the prescription to follow.[7] The eruption of violence that opposes the *banlieue* youth and the police, moreover, has been carefully framed ideologically to seem less like a riot and more like the first battle in a violent political revolution that seeks to overthrow or secede from the French state. Music could be heard speaking of a "coup d'état," and the police had been called an occupying army. And indeed, when the police arrive en masse, they look like a regular military contingent: successive shots show symmetrical lines of armored, shielded men smartly clicking down their helmet visors in rhythmic succession. But the young rioters, interestingly, are never shown to be driven back and dominated as a group. The message is clear—fighting back (even revolt itself) is a real possibility. A similar moment of *banlieue* youths fighting efficaciously against the police would be seen again in *Les savates du bon Dieu* (*Workers for the Good Lord*) (Brisseau, 2000), in which the inhabitants of a *banlieue* housing project rain down large objects on a sizeable police force, put the officers in retreat, and surround them in a wall of flames, all to save three outlaws.

The music that accompanies the scene of battle at the end of *Ma 6-t* also casts the young men less as rioters than as revolutionaries, as the aforementioned rap song "La sédition" (by 2 Bal 2 Neg) suggested (rap is, of course, a key musical genre for youth in France, especially in the suburbs). The clearly audible lyrics and refrain of this song inform us,

6. "Declaration of the Rights of Man and of the Citizen," Constitution of Year I (1793) in *The Constitutions and Other Select Documents Illustrative of the History of France 1789–1901*, ed. and trans. Frank Maloy Anderson (Minneapolis: Wilson, 1904), 174.

7. Jean-François Richet, the film's director, who is, moreover, from the *banlieue*, has denied, unconvincingly, that his film is a call to insurrection. See Michel Cieutat, "*Ma 6-t va crack-er*," *CinémAction* 103 (2002): 201.

and potentially the young people from the *banlieue* who see the film,[8] of what is at stake: "Sedition is the solution, revolution. / Let's multiply the protests, now draw our weapon." Other notable verses include: "Nothing nor no one can snuff out a revolt," "We add up the forces to / face the menace of the bourgeois state," "Open the door of civil war, and come in with pride," and "Just for the pleasure of it, I repeat / *Ma 6-t va crack-er* (My *cité* is gonna crack), a complete revolution." These last verses provide insight into the meaning of the film, by contextualizing its name, "Ma 6-t va crack-er," which could be written more conventionally as "Ma cité va craquer" (My *cité* is going to burst"). The title, at first, could be construed as a warning that if nothing is done, the ghetto-*banlieue* will burst, or break, similar to *La haine*'s warning of "Jusqu'ici, tout va bien" (So far, so good), but in light of the song in which pleasure is taken in announcing this coming bursting of the city, it now reads as gleeful prediction and prescription, rather than as a cautionary tale.

Violent revolution, civil war, things going up in flame, sedition, article 35 of the Declaration of the Rights of Man—this is not the simple imaginary of a riot, but that of the French Revolution itself, to which this struggle in the *banlieue* is compared, in a clear strategy of legitimization.

Lefebvre held that a revolution, if successful, would also produce its own space, and indeed, that reconfiguring space would also be a means by which to carry out the revolution, a way of fighting against the hegemonic forces that until then had generated it (See Lefebvre, 54, 408–12). In this way, in affecting the physical space of the *banlieue*, which they do by punctuating it with burned vehicles and buildings, its inhabitants may be playing a role in producing their own social space and condition, albeit negatively. In the cinema and in the actual suburbs, then, riots can also be considered not merely as reactive delinquency but also as bids for power, or even as nascent revolutions, especially in a nation where revolution is considered legitimate, and is even glorified, both in the school curriculum and in the mainstream press. It should be noted that real-life suburban youth of immigrant origin generally grew up speaking French,[9] having a sense of "being" French, and

8. The film was unofficially censored by theaters, which restricted its release. Many clips of the film, however, and especially of its rap-infused violent end, are currently both available and often viewed on video file-sharing sites such as YouTube and Dailymotion.

9. See Alec Hargreaves and Mark McKinney, "Introduction: The Post-Colonial

wishing to integrate into a society that would live up to what they were taught in the national schools, that is, the ideal of a French Republic in which the race, national origins, and religion of citizens do not matter. When that ideal is violated, quite logically, they look to the historical remedy to extreme injustice also taught in school, namely the Revolution.[10]

The production of space through violence may, however, be counter-productive. According to Gilles Deleuze and Félix Guattari in their *Anti-Oedipus,* capitalism, as it expands, produces newly "deterritorialized" spaces (economic and political configurations characterized by "flows" of labor and capital rather than fixed, archaic relationships to land and State) both in other countries and within a State's borders, *on the periphery.*[11] Here, traditional sectors break down, and inequality in productivity and income becomes extreme, as the periphery is exploited for the benefit of the center.[12] While rioters may be revolting against the signs of an economic system that defines their peripheral existence, the underdeveloped character of the *banlieue* only increases when young men degrade the socio-economic space of the suburb by burning cars and buildings, that is, by multiplying the markers of deterritorialized space that capitalism already imposed: like the actors of so many urban riots, from Paris to Los Angeles, they assist capitalism in generating the very spatial conditions from which they seek escape. Their actions, then, are open to opposing interpretations: as nascent revolutionary violence on the one hand, and as the worsening of a spatial configuration already unfavorable to them on the other.

The film *Jeunesse dorée* (2002), made by a director (Ghorab-Volta) who grew up in the French suburbs and is of Maghrebi origin, also pro-

---

Problematic in France" in *Post-colonial Cultures in France* (London: Routledge, 1997), 19. A 2003 poll of 18–30 year-olds born in France to Maghrebi parents, however, notes a decline since 1993 of stated feelings of appurtenance to French culture. See TNS Sofres, "La marche pour l'égalité, 20 ans après," December 2003 (http://www.tns-sofres.com/etudes/pol/031203_egalite_r.htm).

10. My thanks to Ramla Bédoui for her insights into the motivations of suburban French youths.

11. See Gilles Deleuze and Félix Guattari, *Anti-Oedipus: Capitalism and Schizophrenia,* trans. Robert Hurley et al. (New York: Viking, 1977), 231–32.

12. Theoretician of space Edward Soja similarly states the uneven development under capitalism (which we can see in the French *banlieue*): "The key point is that capitalism . . . intrinsically builds upon regional or spatial inequalities as a necessary means for its continued survival. The very existence of capitalism presupposes the sustaining presence and vital instrumentality of geographically uneven development." Edward Soja, *Postmodern Geographies* (London: Verso, 1989), 107.

vides a particularly productive look at the space of the *banlieue,* both
in its lucid diagnosis of the political causes that generated that space,
and in its imaginary of destruction. Though the film seems less harsh
than other *banlieue* films, the destruction shown is actually even more
thorough. The movie begins in a typical French suburb, and focuses on
two very young (white) women who live there, Angela and Gwen, best
friends who apply for a grant with a local association to document isolated buildings in rural locations throughout France.

The trip they undertake shows us that the suburb is not limited to
the space of the suburb, that is, that the *cité* housing projects that have
come to define the *banlieue* are not actually always in a suburb, but
rather are sometimes placed in the middle of the countryside. The
young women arrive in what looks to be a typical, modern graffitied
*cité,* but one in fact bordered by a rural landscape (with no nearby city
center visible); the contrast is emphasized as the women sit down at
the visual border between *cité* and countryside, against a concrete wall
behind and next to which a green recreational space gives way to even
more verdant hills and trees. Their encounter with the young men of
North African origin who live there goes smoothly, in a sequence
marked by human warmth, welcoming, friendly attitudes, kindness,
and respect, providing a counterexample to the *cité* as a dangerous, hostile place. Unlike the racially-tinged stereotypes prevalent in France,
they meet neither with violence nor sexual intimidation.

Exposing and highlighting the rural location of this and similar developments points out that the *cité,* and, by extension the *banlieue*
with which it is heavily identified, is not a spatial problem. Rather than
a natural, "organic" outgrowth of a dense urban core on the borders of
which it just crops up, the *cité* and the *banlieue* are a political choice,
deliberately and artificially isolated from the city. We see this also
when Angela and Gwen take note of a middle-aged woman walking
alone on a busy highway, who indicates that the housing development
is in one direction, and the supermarket to where she is headed, far in
another: even the most basic necessity of food has been strangely and
artificially isolated from the suburban residential spaces.

Angela and Gwen soon come across a very sizeable mid-rise housing project similarly placed in a rural setting, the implosion of which a
crowd has gathered to witness. The elevated location from which they
watch the building fall, at a distance, shows that the people clearly
dominate the situation and space now, and the imploding building pro-
vokes the cheers and applause of the crowd. *Jeunesse dorée* first gives

us, then, the clear diagnosis that what had seemed a spatial problem is, in fact, a political choice of separation, and then proposes a political and spatial solution to it: destroy it.

The position of *Jeunesse dorée* in this regard is close to that of Mustafa Dikeç, who has argued that the *banlieue* does not exist, other than as a notion to mask in and through space what is essentially a political problem, and to justify a policy of containment by positing certain populations as Other (elsewhere in space and different, dangerous in nature).[13] The *banlieue* then, is not the problem, but rather the political and racist causes (such as an oppressive state and larger society) that gave rise to it and that continue to sustain it.

Unlike in *La haine*, which was structured around a radical dichotomy between Paris and the *banlieue*, in this road movie that is *Jeunesse dorée*, as well as in *Ma 6-t*, there are no trips to Paris as there are in so many *banlieue* films.[14] Here the suburbs no longer look to the city, nor symbolically to the political and economic power that Paris represents.

## MOMENTS OF *BANLIEUE* OPTIMISM

With a growing indifference to or disillusionment with the city, one might expect filmic attempts at more positive evaluations of suburban space, and there are some small signs of this. After the rather spectacular demolition in *Jeunesse dorée*, for example, the two young women interview two former inhabitants, a mother and daughter who provide a counterpoint to the celebration of destruction: they are physically shocked to lose these places imbued with their past and their memories, and that, for them, formed a "village" of multicultural *entente* and familial ties. There are also positive portrayals of the suburb in *100% Arabica* (*100% Arabic*) (Zemmouri, 1997), in which the *banlieue* appears often as a place filled with joyous (raï) music and dancing, which

13. See Mustafa Dikeç, "Police, Politics, and the Right to the City," *GeoJournal* 58 (2002): 91–98.

14. For the trip motif in *banlieue* cinema, and for how the spatial relation of characters to the suburb and city in *La haine* is created by using different focal lengths and film gauges, and through narrative technique, see Myrto Konstantarakos, "What Mapping of the City? *La Haine* and the *cinéma du banlieue*," in *French Cinema in the 1990s* (Oxford: Oxford University Press, 1999), 160–71, esp. 162. For the physical and social space of the suburb in *La haine*, and for the film's "aesthetic" qualities, see Ginette Vincendeau, "Designs on the *banlieue*: Mathieu Kassovitz's *La haine*," in *French Film: Texts and Contexts* (London: Routledge, 2000), 310–27.

are used to fight against religious fundamentalism. The spaces associated with the music are simultaneously open to the air and cozily surrounded by a grouping of neighborhood buildings that form a loose
courtyard, seemingly echoing the community that spontaneously
flocks around the space as soon as the singing and playing begin. This
free-form space contrasts with the strict, closed space of the funda-
mentalist mosque, which loses the fight for the heart of the community. In a rare moment for the *banlieue* cinema, the inhabitants
have taken over and created their own positive space here, albeit
only ephemerally. *L'esquive* (*Games of Love and Chance*) (Abdellatif
Kechiche, 2003) also features a sometimes positive representation of
the *banlieue*, but less for the place itself than for the human experience
that occurs there, as suburban high-school students rehearse a play by
eighteenth-century author Marivaux, with for a backdrop the ever-
present *barres*. Even a film featuring the graffiti-tagged, drug-ridden,
dystopic *banlieue* as does *Wesh Wesh, qu'est-ce qui se passe?*, shows
us seductive nighttime representations of an illuminated *banlieue*, the
camera panning over lit-up buildings that shine at us with beauty, mys-
tery, and hopefulness.

In terms of *banlieue* optimism, the case of *Banlieue 13* (*District 13*)
(Morel, 2004) is a curious mix, radically dystopian at the film's beginning, and radically utopian at film's end. This hybrid film—part *banlieue* movie, part action flick, and almost science-fiction—features a
*cité* that by 2010 has become a lawless camp surrounded by barbed
wire, one walled-off by the French state, and in which a bomb sent by
the French government is supposed to kill the two million residents
who live there (so that as a French government official tells us, other
citizens need neither fear them nor pay for their social services). The
ending of the film shows us another fantasy, this time utopian: the gov-
ernment-sponsored genocide is averted through the efforts of two male
heroes who are fierce defenders of the core values of the French Republic. The film concludes in a triumph of democracy, of the freedom
of the press, and of the importance of that central value of the French
Republic, *égalité*, especially as it pertains to the equality of all citizens
before the law. In the end, this seemingly radical film pictures less destruction than *Jeunesse dorée*, but *Banlieue 13* is exceptionally pre-
scient: it shows the high ranking French government official referring
to the inhabitants of the suburb as *racaille* (scum), just after he attempted to genocidally bomb them, and while the slur now sounds
quite familiar, the film was released in 2004, one year before then-Min-

ister of the Interior Nicolas Sarkozy spoke (25 October 2005) of ridding the banlieue of its, again, *racaille*. Sarkozy's words did a great deal to (literally) inflame an explosive situation in Clichy-sous-Bois, the suburb of Paris where two days after Sarkozy spoke, two youths died, electrocuted as they fled the police, and the suburbs began to burn.

## GREATER PARIS

We find an urban and suburban imaginary perhaps not so much optimistic as nostalgic in *Les triplettes de Belleville*. While many will recall its vision of cities, the film's representation of the suburb is more fleeting, nearly absent, and that is exactly what is interesting about it. It refuses to show any sort of suburb, even when by realist conventions it could and should. This animated film is not particularly bound by realism, but its choices and imaginary world do reveal the non-place that the suburb is held to be.

At the beginning of the film, after we have been introduced to the protagonists—Mme Souza, her grandson Champion, and their dog Bruno—a sequence highlights the changing space around their home. It is clearly located in a rural space: the isolated, two-storey house of average size is surrounded by fields. Successive shots show the world around the house changing, as the seasons and the years pass. To the tragic strains of Mozart's Great Mass in C minor, the city, at first very far-off, creeps nearer; a few scattered houses appear, and then increase in number and density as Paris and its construction cranes draw nearer to their abode (the cranes provide a neat visual rhyme with a more distant Eiffel Tower in a way that also brings that structure and its symbolism forward). While we see the countryside and later the city in several shots, the intermediate stage of something resembling a suburb is transitory, fleeting, barely present at all aside from, at the most, two shots, lasting approximately 10 seconds. The imaginary of the suburb is that of its near-invisibility, and then its rapid disappearance, as it is quickly integrated into the urban core. At the end of the sequence, the city of Paris has engulfed the countryside.

An elevated metro passes just outside the second floor of their home, which seems to lean back from the intrusive rail line. In the process, a rather idyllic rural setting, inundated with sunshine and warm colors (yellows, orange . . .) has given way to a somewhat dystopic urban setting, colored a cold grey-blue tinged with green where it seems to rain constantly, and where the streets resemble an underworld fa-

miliar to us from the constantly drizzling subterranean street spaces of
*Blade Runner* (Ridley Scott, 1982). The countryside has become city,
much as the rural village Montmartre joined Paris, though unlike with
Montmartre, which retained some of its village feel, here that comes at
a high cost, that of dystopia.

While Paris stopped expanding its borders in the mid-nineteenth
century, and no longer annexed new territory into Parisian space, in *Les
triplettes* this process has continued: on the side of a bus that passes
near the characters' home (which is now located in Paris), one can read
that it stops at the "Mairie du XXIᵉ," or the city hall of the twenty-first
*arrondissement* (district) of Paris, which, of course, in reality currently
only has twenty (sacrosanct) *arrondissements*. We are given a cinematic idea of what to do with the suburbs: make them disappear into
city space, by expanding the boundaries of Paris itself to include them.

Another revealing moment in *Les triplettes* comes as Champion,
his grandmother, and the triplets escape from the city of Belleville and
from the French mafia gangsters who are in pursuit of them, and take
a very industrial-looking bridge (similar to the Queensborough bridge
in New York City), crossing from the ultra-urbanized (beautiful) Belleville directly into the forlorn, dark countryside. What is striking is that
it is immediately rural: one might expect an urban environment on the
other side of the river from a city that is a mix of New York, Paris, Mon-
treal, and San Francisco, or at least a suburban configuration, but that
is not the case. The suburban is excluded from the very imaginary of
this film, which harkens back to an older, more traditional city/coun-
tryside divide that has long resonated in the French cultural and cinematic sphere.[15]

The *Triplettes* constitutes, after all, a very nostalgic vision of
France, replete with berets and accordions (to the point of caricature)
and sometimes mild critique. This rural space on the other side of the
bridge is a place of escape and escapism, as the characters are propelled
there by Champion's cinema-bike machine for projecting completely
realistic images of the Tour de France bicycle race, in striking contrast
to the rest of the animated world of *Les triplettes*. The bicycle-powered
platform suddenly becomes a mobile cinema capable of outrunning
even the Mafioso's numerous black automobiles, as it is pedaled by

15. Even Mme Souza's brief moments on the outskirts of Belleville, before she is
taken in by the triplets, are spent in what looks much more like a nineteenth-century
*faubourg* than a modern suburb.

Champion, long enslaved to this machine, and focused on the screen ahead on which he sees images of the countryside and villages, passing by as they might from the point of view of a cyclist. Lost in a Matrix-like cinematic immersion in the ideal world of that most typical of French events, the Tour de France, he escapes into the countryside of France, one that is definitely without a suburb.

## THE UTOPIA OF DESTRUCTION (CONCLUSIONS)

The urban/suburban imaginary explored above tends to point to the radical solution of obliterating the suburb altogether. This is likely a politically aware longing coming out of a *banlieue* that has diagnosed the political and economic causes of the problem, as the case of *Ma 6-t* and *Jeunesse dorée* seems to indicate, and it also may be a function of a cultural sphere that refuses the *banlieue* and privileges the city, as the case of *Les triplettes* suggests.

These films are also, it should be noted, efforts to produce a revolution in space, both by showing us how space is constituted, and by suggesting the elimination of the suburbs, whether by pure absorption into urban space, by seditious separation (by damaging and burning), or by the simple destruction of the emblematic mid-rise *banlieue barres* themselves. This is indeed a spatial imaginary, though a negative one: we have not yet reached the point where the cinema presents us with what a new, well-urbanized *banlieue* might look like, or with an attractive vision of a place where lower-income residents or the unemployed might live. In other words, the *banlieue* films and their characters do generate their own space, but mostly by destroying what is there, and not by creating some new, durable spatial organization inscribed in the (sub)urban fabric. A purely negative spatial imaginary, however, is not entirely to be lamented, as the real answer to the *banlieue* likely does not lie in creating a space that concentrates minority or lower income populations in one place, however pleasant, but rather in eliminating those concentrations, and in finding structural economic and political answers to the problems residents face, wherever they live.

MARGARET C. FLINN

# Signs of the Times: Chris Marker's *Chats perchés*

> Nothing surprising about a cat on a roof. But a yellow and black cat measuring—so far as one could tell from street-level—a good three meters, that is, the whole height of the chimney's flank? A resolutely grinning cat, one determined to keep his grin . . . a grin that seemed equally determined not to leave the cat. Cat without a grin, grin without a cat, out of the question, all of that. The cat and the grin were one.
> —François Maspero, "Les chats de la liberté"[1]

> *Chats perchés* is an event, and must be received as such.
> —François Lecointe, in *L'esprit*[2]

Like Chris Marker's CD-ROM *Immemory* and his 212 postings in 2004 as Guillaume-en-Egypte[3] on the graphic art blog *unregardmoderne*, his film *Chats perchés* (*The Case of the Grinning Cat*) (2004) explores and politicizes relationships among sound, image, and text within the context of new media, practicing digital collage in an explicitly international forum. While collecting instances of "found" words, the film also collects its eponymous cats: the graffiti'd "Monsieur Chat," who had been appearing in death-defying locations across the Parisian landscape, and spreading to the internet and cities worldwide. M. Chat is an icon of eccentric, lyrical intervention into the webs of 21st-century social space—crossing from street, to newspaper, to film, to gallery, to television, to the internet, and back again.

1. First published in *Thématiques*, special issue of *La nouvelle vie ouvrière* (December 2003). This citation is from page 9 of the bonus booklet accompanying the DVD of *Chats perchés*. All translations appearing in this article are my own. I owe thanks to Sam Di Iorio, Bill Horrigan, and Jim Austin for helping keep me informed of new M. Chat sightings, and other timely suggestions.
2. François Lecointe, "Grinning cats . . . à propos de *Chats perchés* de Chris Marker," *Esprit* 311 (January 2005): 177.
3. A pseudonym and cartoon ginger tabby long used by Marker in honor of his now deceased pet.

**YFS 115,** *New Spaces for French and Francophone Cinema*, ed. James F. Austin, © 2009 by Yale University.

This article will examine *Chats perchés*'s reception, and then look at the film in relation to notions of the figural, the digitextual, and the event, concluding with a discussion of the meeting of art and politics through M. Chat in the context of digital culture. Through *Chats perchés* and its attendant media events, Chris Marker's engagement with the post-graffiti street art cat re-actualizes questions about the arbitrariness and mutability of signs fundamental to 20th-century documentary filmmaking by posing them in the context of 21st-century media convergence.

## "BETWEEN REAL POLITICS AND FELINE UTOPIA"[4]

The product of Chris Marker's digital video perambulations through the streets of Paris from late 2001 through 2003, the 59 minute *Chats perchés* was co-produced by the Franco-German television station Arte and officially premiered on December 4, 2004 in Arte's documentary series, *La lucarne*. In spite of *La lucarne*'s Saturday midnight time slot, *Chats perchés* hardly slipped by unnoticed: it had advanced screenings on December 3 at the Centre Pompidou as well as two free screenings at the Bibliothèque Nationale on December 5. The film and the events surrounding its release caught the attention of a broad range of press, from the popular *Le Parisien* to the Catholic intellectual journal *L'esprit* (including nearly all the major dailies in between). *Chats perchés* also enjoyed excellent and numerous on-line reviews of the DVD, as well as mentions on blogs of "crazy cat people" by counterculturally-inclined fans of street art and film festival goers. Since its premier weekend, the film has traveled from the festival circuit (Torino to Macau) to art house release in major cities.[5] It has also been the subject of a steady and overwhelmingly positive stream of print and blog reviews everywhere it has appeared.

The bright yellow, broad-grinned feline M. Chat first appeared on

---

4. Jacques Mandelbaum, "[Culture Cinéma: Chats perchés de Chris Marker] Un appel à la poésie, entre POLITIQUE réelle et UTOPIE féline: Un bilan lucide d'un monde en proie à la folie et à l'injustice," *Le monde* (December 1, 2004): 29.

5. By the time of its United States theatrical release in December 2006, the film had already enjoyed archive screenings, such as multiple dates at the Gene Siskal Film Center in Chicago (June 2006), in addition to festival appearances. It is also featured in the 2007–08 selection for the French-American Cultural Exchange *Tournées* Grant program, which subsidizes showings on several American campuses in the context of French film festivals.

the French street art scene in Orléans in 1997 (Figure 1). He rapidly spread to Paris and most provincial French cities. At the time of this writing he has been documented in locations as far flung as Sarajevo and the Brazilian Nordeste.[6] Although he started as a ground-level creation, the speed with which he was erased by street cleaners caused him quickly to be moved to rooftop perches (hence the "perched cats" of the film's French title).[7] Created by an anonymous collective (who also call themselves M. Chat), M. Chat has since been appropriated by anyone willing to risk his or her neck to paint him.

In late 2001, Marker began filming the cat's various appearances on the walls of the capital, but at the time of the 2002 French presidential elections the project took a hard turn toward the political. The film's two strands (the feline and the political) join after about 20 minutes, during the second round of the presidential elections, when, with obvious delight, Marker's camera glimpses the cat over the shoulder of a television newscaster, Place de la Bastille, in a new manifestation as a signboard in the rally. In an interview with the national daily *Libération*, Marker comments on this shift in focus from Parisian street art to contemporary street politics:

[*Libération* interviewer Annick Rivoire]: The filmed stroll, conceived in a positive light, took a pessimistic turn . . .

C. M.: Everything changed with the second round of the elections. I had followed the first anti-Le Pen demonstrations on May 1 . . . But all of a sudden on my T.V. screen, behind PPDA, *the grinning cat* [in English in the original] himself . . . I flung myself into the metro, trying to figure out where I could catch up with the demonstration.[8]

The conjuncture of the two previously separate areas, in fact, only occurs on screen at the moment when M. Chat appears, on television, in the election-related demonstration. However, much of the demonstra-

6. Photos available on the Google Maps tool of http://monsieurchat.free.fr/Mchat.php (consulted December 11, 2006). Monsieurchat.free.fr is the most comprehensive site documenting M. Chat sightings, although its mapping feature (using Google Maps) is relatively new and includes fewer photos than can be found on various blogs and photosharing sites.

7. Ngoc Loan Lam, "Chats alors! Les chats d'Orléans font des petits en France," *La Nouvelle République du Centre-Ouest* (August 8, 2005): 111.

8. PPDA is Patrick Poivre d'Arvor, French writer, journalist, television news anchor, and media personality. Chris Marker and M. Chat, interview by Annick Rivoire, "Chats discutent," *Libération* (December 4, 2004): 26–27.

*Figure 1.* M. Chat in two of his manifestations on Parisian walls. Top: still from *Chats perchés,* courtesy of Icarus Films. Bottom: photograph courtesy Patrick M. Bray.

tion footage that appears in *Chats perchés* would have been shot well before the elections—most notably the anti-war demonstrations of March 2002. Thus, Marker's filming of quotidian Paris had already become "sidetracked" into political demonstrations before the incident that he claims shifted his focus from the cat to the demonstrations. In light of this slippage, one wonders if Marker has not simply appropriated M. Chat for his own ends. But what ends?

Within the film's scant hour, its narrative ricochets dizzyingly between domestic and international, between demonstrations massive and marginal, and among as many subjects as there are demonstrations. Marker's rapid-fire montage encourages confusion, mixing documentary images with playful creations (M. Chat as a stamp, M. Chat in canonical works of art) until it emerges that in *Chats perchés*, politics is as much about the *"faits divers"* (minor news items) as about "the cause." The proliferation of demonstrations, their fragmentation and their ultimately unclear meaning establish a tone of melancholic idealism that, I would argue, accounts for *Chats perchés*'s success in tapping into a deep sense of ambivalence and contradiction currently affecting French national identity. *Chats perchés* is in fact very much about "the signs of the times," both political and artistic.

French and North American reviewers alike shared a lexicon of positive terms to describe the film: whimsical, playful, mischievous, organic, free-associative, witty, daydreamy, poetic, puckish, refreshing, sly, charming, graceful, even-handed, wry, poignant, *insoumise* (insubordinate). And critics of all kinds were equally impressed with Marker's vitality, and the film's ability to wed the ludic feline to the deadly serious politics of 2001–2. The connection to Marker's 1977 *Le fond de l'air est rouge (Grin without a Cat)* was recognized even in France before the film's English title was announced, as *Télérama's* Jérémie Couston joked that "For Chris Marker, the air is tinted yellow ["le fond de l'air est jaune"] and beauty is in the Paris streets. Meow!"[9]

The frequently observed connection between the 1977 and 2004

9. Jérémie Couston, "Chats perchés," *Télérama* (December 4–10 2005): 103. Other reviewers who explicitly made the connection included Emmanuel Chicon in *L'humanité*, Manohla Dargis of the *New York Times*, Chris Darke in *Film Comment*, J. Hoberman of the *Village Voice*, Eric Henderson, *Slant Magazine*, Ray Greene of *Boxoffice.com*, Karina Longworth of *Cinematical.com*, Matt Peterson of *The Brooklyn Rail*, and the anonymous reviewer of the *Onion A. V. Club*.

films[10] certainly makes sense in terms of the attempt to chronicle a period and its disillusionments, but *Grin Without a Cat* maintains the integrity of each of the events it treats in a way that *Chats* does not. The sheer heft of three hours versus one certainly contributes to this difference. But what is truly different here is that while Marker's work has always skillfully pointed out the contradictions and paradoxes of political and cultural discourses, after *Chats perchés,* one wonders if there remains anything *but* contradictions and paradoxes. There certainly is a tiredness in this film that Eric Henderson of *Slant Magazine* calls "unmistakably a piece of old man cinema, a sadder-but-wiser companion piece to the likes of *A Prairie Home Companion, I'm Going Home,* and *Gertrud.*"[11]

Indeed the film itself holds up a suggestive mirror to Marker when the hitherto rapid montage settles on a lingering portrait of a white-haired leftist at the 2002 May Day/anti-LePen protests: punctuated by a freeze frame, the man flashes a "V for victory" sign with his left hand. "How many May Days in his memory?" reads the intertitle spliced in the middle of the medium close-up. The image and title-card are among the most suggestively nostalgic of the film, as of course voting for Chirac would be anything but a victorious act for an *habitué* of the May Day parade. One is tempted to see in this older gentleman a stand-in for Marker himself, "au courant while lost in the past," as J. Hoberman characterizes the director.[12]

## FIGURING M. CHAT

The appeal of M. Chat's smile, floating above the urban jungle, is anchored in its lyrical deformation of the everyday environment. *Chats perchés* is a film about many such deformations and distortions, of both

10. See Manohla Dargis, "Leftist Politics Scampers Through Paris on Playful Paws" *New York Times* (December 20, 2006), http://movies2.nytimes.com/2006/12/20/movies/20grin.html (consulted December 22, 2006); Karina Longworth, "Tribeca Review: The Case of the Grinning Cats [sic]," posted April 30, 2006, 2:00 pm, http://www.cinematical.com/2006/04/30/tribeca-review-the-case-of-the-grinning-cats/(consulted June 24, 2006); Review of *Onion A. V. Club,* http://avclub.com/content/node/56846 (consulted January 18, 2007).

11. Eric Henderson, Review of *The Case of the Grinning Cat, Slant Magazine,* http://www.slantmagazine.com/film/film_review.asp?ID=2722 (consulted January 18, 2007).

12. J. Hoberman, "Cat Power: Chris Marker and his feline friend document post-9-11 France," *The Village Voice,* posted December 19, 2006, 4:11 pm, http://www.villagevoice.com/film/0651,hoberman,75338,20.html (consulted January 18, 2007).

spaces and meanings. Some of these deformations are simply recorded by Marker—that is, *Chats perchés* does include sequences with a nearly straightforward representational agenda: to document M. Chat's presence on city walls. Yet the primary deformation of signification in *Chats perchés* originates in cinematic or multimedia technique. Marker here works both on the audio and visual registers—and quite powerfully on the interactions between the two.

To take only the most striking case of vertical montage challenging and disquieting the viewer, I would turn to the sequence documenting a "lie-in" at the Champs de Mars in protest of the French (and other Western) government's lack of an adequate anti-AIDS policy. In this relatively lengthy sequence, the haunting melody from the soundtrack of Alain Resnais's *Hiroshima mon amour* (1959) plays over stills of the demonstrators. While the soundtrack references the post-apocalyptic *Hiroshima*, the image track of stills is reminiscent of Marker's own post-apocalyptic masterpiece, *La jetée* (1962): the *Chats* images start in color, but then pass to black and white, transitioning at the same careful pace. The AIDS demonstration images consist of bodies lying down, dressed lightly for the warm weather, suggesting a strange conjugation of the two most famous passages of *Hiroshima* and *La jetée:* the opening of *Hiroshima* where the intertwined bodies of the lovers are shown in the near-abstraction of close-up and the single moving image of *La jetée* of the reclining woman (the main character's love). The juxtaposition of 1959, 1962, 2002, and their respective representations of history within the 2004 film demand that the viewer compare and contrast, considering the disturbing similarities and—one hopes— thinking through the specificities of each series of events, while implicitly opening the question of the ethics of such comparisons.

The ghostly movement introduced in *La jetée* would, in the CD-ROM *Immemory*, take a form now familiar to Marker connoisseurs as the "Morph-eye" graphic. The Morph-eye takes an existing image and manipulates it digitally, adding an eerie movement to the figure by using a limited number of frames. In *Chats perchés*, George Bush falls several times under the gaze of the Morph-eye, as do politicians and commentators of the French presidential election. In these sequences, the digital transformation of the image emphasizes the artifices of discourse, drawing attention to what in hindsight appears as ridiculous miscalculation, for example the bold rhetoric on the French extreme left of Green Party leader Noël Mamère, who stated "It is to take the French for idiots to suggest that Jospin could possibly *not* be in the second round," or deliberate falsification, as with the U.S. battleship infamously hung with the proclamation "Mission Accomplished."

*Chats perchés'* self-reflexive montage deformation of information thus reminds its viewers that history is never unmediated. While a faux White House website sporting M. Chat is one of a series of digital collages, Marker also includes images of at least two *real* websites in his inventory of the grinning cat's appearance. The film thus veers between information, disinformation, and counterinformation, often willfully confounding, moreover, the viewer's expectations. In the election sequence, for instance, suspense is built by showing election posters, various bits of reportage, speech-making and other election-related material, yet the first images after the title card that reads "April 21st, the catastrophe" are of the bandaged paw of a cat named Boléro, the companion of a young homeless woman who appears several times throughout the film. Whether or not Boléro actually got his paw caught in the escalator on April 21 is, of course, irrelevant. Given Marker's penchant for multilingual word play, the catastrophe of the election must somehow also be a cat-astrophe, thus calling into question received ideas or assumptions about events.

This combinatory word play, requiring the image of Boléro to emphasize the first syllable of "catastrophe," suggests the usefulness of David Rodowick's definition of the figural, as laid out in his *Reading the Figural, or, Philosophy after the New Media*, for explicating *Chats perchés*.[13] Using the work of Jean-François Lyotard as a springboard, Rodowick defines the figural as a concept which allows one to avoid opposing—and hierarchizing—the linguistic and the plastic, word and image, verbal and visual. For Rodowick, the figural is "a semiotic regime where the ontological distinction between linguistic and plastic representations breaks down . . . [and] a transformation of discourse by recent technologies of the visible" (Rodowick, 2). Rodowick does not mean to suggest that the figural does not exist before new media, but rather that "in their own peculiar transformations of discourse, the new media help us challenge in new ways the ontological gesture that separates the arts of time from the arts of space" (Rodowick, 4). The great advantage, then, of Rodowick's argument is that the visual need no longer be "banished from the realm of discourse" (Rodowick, 4)— that is, discourse is not limited to the linguistic.

---

13. D. N. Rodowick, *Reading the Figural, or, Philosophy after the New Media* (Durham, NC: Duke UP, 2001).

Rodowick's grouping of the "figural" allows us to see how both words and images signify within urban space, and within the filmed representation of that space. Peeling apart the layers of urban semiosis, Marker reforms quotidian texts into a series of diegetic intertitles—the swirling of a projector on the floor of a shopping arcade cues viewers that the film has reached the turn of the New Year (2002), while "*Vigilance—propreté*" (Vigilence—cleanliness) on the plastic bag of the city's green garbage repositories wryly comments upon the election campaign posters that precede it. The central deformation operational in *Chats perchés* is thus the experience of city space itself. To borrow a term from Tom Conley, the city has a "graphic unconscious" that *Chats perchés* brings to the fore by including representatives of all the following textual signifying systems: newspapers, poster advertising, subway station names, street signs, all-over bus ads, t-shirts, lightboards, projection systems, campaign posters, movie posters, maps, candy machines, television screens, websites, protest stickers, buttons and signs, tag graffiti, stencil graffiti, murals, and a wide variety of what art historians are calling post-graffiti street art.[14] The latter include the Space Invaders and Jérôme Mesnager figures familiar to Parisian pedestrians, as well as another allusion to the cinema by means of an image of sticker street art affixed to a Lancôme ad featuring actor-director Mathieu Kassovitz. Like the M. Chat collective, these contemporary street artists move among street, gallery, and internet art spaces.

Marker uses both word and image to signal European and French responses to American foreign policy by following the "Mission Accomplished" banner and an American general's press conference with a telling series of shots. First, an upside-down, screaming woman's face from a subway ad campaign, then the "Europe" metro station name plaque, and finally an ad-campaign reproduction of Delacroix's *Liberty Leading the People* are all glimpsed through the palimpsest created by the windows of passing subway trains. Only if the viewer can understand the advertising image of the screaming woman, the allegorical Delacroix reproduction, and the word "Europe" as each having equal signifying force—that is, as a figurative ensemble—can this sequence become truly readable.

M. Chat himself bridges the same word/image barrier—moreover, he embodies the attributes that Rodowick argues are shared by the fig-

14. Tom Conley, *The Graphic Unconscious in Early Modern French Writing* (New York, Cambridge UP, 1992).

ural and the Freudian unconscious: "the absence of negation or contradiction; extreme mobility of libidinal energy and intensity of cathexes; intemporality and concomitance of the pleasure principle" (14). The figural then can be conceptualized by looking at the free play of the cat through *Chats perchés*. Not only is M. Chat shown in multiple poses and in multiple media, but in fact images of various other felines appear, set in resonance to M. Chat—implying that they are and yet are not him (a cat is a cat is a cat, as it were). There are stencil and tag graffiti cats, poster-cats for shelters, mummified cats in the Louvre, and several real-life cats.

In addition, Marker and the collective that paints M. Chat, have emphasized that "Chat" functions verbally as well as visually, suggesting two possible acronyms to apply to their collaboration in the *Chats perchés* premier events and, in fact, to M. Chat when painted by anyone: the *Communauté Harmonieuse des Artistes Taciturnes* (The Harmonious Community of Taciturn Artists) and the *Conféderation Humaniste et Anarchiste des Travailleurs* (the Humanist and Anarchist Confederation of Workers). The cat as "word" is further emphasized by thinking of M. Chat as a category under which to search on the Internet—a problem that Marker illustrates in the film through a quick image of a search engine results page: the linguistic co-incidence of "chat" as cat in French and as the French and English terms for discussion in chat rooms turn up a large number of irrelevant results!

But above all, for Marker, the cat (the animal) is that which is the un-co-optable, the irrecuperable, the inappropriable:

> the cat, the only being in the world who—from time immemorial—captured his place in the foreground of daily life, of the image, of feeling, and of mythology, without ever having been appropriated or co-opted. Prévert said it better than anyone: "They insulted the cows / They insulted the gorillas / the chickens / They insulted the calves / they insulted the geese [*les serins*] / the pigs the mackerels / the camels / They insulted dogs / The cats / They didn't dare. (Marker, *Libèration*, 26–27)

Citing the entirety of Jacques Prévert's "Cataire," Marker insists upon the sovereignty of the animal, its resistance to human domination. The cat was thus the perfect emblem for an artistic intervention intended to be appropriable in a positive sense, by anyone wishing to paint him. M. Chat's spokesperson, Thoma Vuille of the Galerie Wall, an Orléans gallery that represents over a dozen emerging artists' collectives, including M. Chat, has stated in interviews that the appropriation of

M. Chat was an intended consequence of the simple style in which the cat is painted: "Anyone should be able to draw this cat, and appropriate him for themselves" (Lam, 111).

## THE DIGITEXTUAL EVENT

One might fairly contend that nothing about *Chats perchés'* filmic language is necessarily radically "new," either for Marker or for film. Rather, *Chats* is a capstone work, combining threads of Marker's introspective early shorts, his political documentary work from the 60s and 70s, and his embrace of multimedia/new media art from the 80s and 90s. It is not the first time Marker has created such a summum. In *Memories of the Future*, Catherine Lupton charts reuse, recurrence, revisitation, and recycling across Marker's œuvre in its many genres and media.[15] For scholars of communication, the primary theorization of the evolving technologies of audio-visual, multimedia, new media and, most recently, digital culture occurs under the blanket term of "media convergence," generally referring to the technological ability to deliver identical digital content across several platforms as well as the corporate synergies and marketing strategies that are attendant on and benefit from those technologies (for example, a music video or a film trailer available via video iPod, MTV, cell phone, and computer). Henry Jenkins has expanded this notion to what he calls "cultural convergence," meaning by this the possibility of convergent narrative structures. A company thus sells a portion of a greater storytelling venture via the medium best adapted to the specific segment or style of narrative.[16]

I would argue that convergence must be discussed in terms of form in order to maintain the possibility for a critical positioning vis-à-vis rapid co-option of digital culture for financial gain and political control. In this light, Chris Marker's *Chats perchés* reactualizes long-standing aesthetic and political questions at the point of convergence between old and new media. In her consideration of convergence, Anna Everett has called "digitextuality" a

15. Catherine Lupton, *Chris Marker: Memories of the Future* (London: Reaktion, 2005).

16. For a concise, journalistic account of technological, economic, social or organic, global, and cultural convergences, see Jenkins's "Digital Renaissance" column titled "Convergence? I Diverge," *Technology Review* (June 2001): 93. Also see Henry Jenkins, *Convergence Culture* (New York: NYU Press, 2006).

metasignifying system of discursive absorption whereby different signifying systems and materials are translated and often transformed into
zeroes and ones for infinite recombinant signifiers. In other words, new
digital media technologies make meaning not only by building a new
text through absorption and transformation of other texts, but also by
embedding the entirety of other texts (analog and digital) seamlessly
within the new.[17]

Within its narrative, *Chats perchés* includes representations of almost
all media and communications technologies currently available, often
via multiple embeddings that foreground the capacity of digital media
to assimilate other media, and literalize Everett's definition. For instance, Marker films a television screen (the edges visible within the
film's frame) on which a television journalist is holding up the front
page of a newspaper. Or in another case, a shot of a flyer dissolves to a
shot of a screen with an electronic version of the same document, while
the document is read aloud by a computer-generated voice.

Meanwhile, the film's release, distribution, and reception have similarly operated on converging planes—mobilizing new and old media
interconnectedly (Figure 2). On December 3, 2004, Marker's entry on
the counterinformation website *unregardmoderne* was an image of
"The Biggest Cat in the World"—the enormous M. Chat drawn by in-
vitation on the Beaubourg piazza by the M. Chat collective. For the
week preceding the preview of *Chats perchés* at the Pompidou, the
Chat collective had also been invited to put 150 cardboard M. Chats
inside the museum, library, and lobby areas of the building itself. On
December 4, the notoriously reclusive Marker joined M. Chat in collaborating on a joint cover-story issue of the newspaper *Libération*
(which they called *Libé-chat-ion*). Besides an extensive double interview and several shorter stories, the issue was designed so that the
pages could be separated and then taped together like a puzzle to form
a flying M. Chat—complete with instructions. Readers were encouraged to tape together M. Chat-Libé, post him somewhere, photograph
him, and then send the photographs back to *Libération*. Moreover, a
flashmob was organized to precede the first screening of *Chats perchés*,
where some 400 flashmobbers assembled on the Pompidou Center
piazza, meowing while walking along the outlines of the gigantic

17. Anna Everett "Digitextuality and Click Theory: Theses on Convergence Media
in the Digital Age," in *New Media: Theories and Practices of Digitextuality*, ed. Anna
Everett and John T. Calwell (New York: Routledge, 2003), 7.

*Figure 2.* "The Biggest Cat in the World." Courtesy Icarus Films.

M. Chat—an annular movement echoing the film's opening scene, which documents flashmobbers circling the golden flower pot sculpture in front of the Center.[18] The "world's biggest cat" flashmob was filmed live by the Center's webcams and diffused via their official site.[19]

On December 5, Marker's *unregardmoderne* entry included the *Libération* cover image. Subsequent to the opening weekend, the already numerous on-line appearances of M. Chat in various blogs and photo-sharing sites (e.g. Flickr and Webshots) began including photos of M. Chat-Libé, and eventually, screen captures from *Chats perchés* also appeared on these sites. Many such sites, particularly the blogs, are linked to monsieurchat.free.fr (a site which chronicles both actual and virtual appearances not only of M. Chat but of Space Invaders and Mesnager figures), which, naturally, re-connected surfers to *unregardmoderne* and the original *Libération* story.

From this brief chronology, then, it should be clear that *Chats perchés* tries to do much more than involve a television audience; it puts in motion a series of interconnected networks of nearly indistinguishable actors and audiences: anyone who paints M. Chat, anyone who tapes together the "chat" issue of *Libération*, anyone who photographs any of these cats, anyone who posts those photographs to the web, anyone who links to any of the other sites. What Marker and M. Chat put into operation is something we might call the digitextual event. The space of the event stretches across virtual and actual spaces, new and old media. This digitextual event includes the instantaneity that is part of the fantasy of the wired world, through the on-line diffusion of the "meatspace" event throughout cyberspace. But it also extends the event from a moment ripped from time, into an event in potentially perpetual re-happening. The *numérique* (digital) thus becomes not simply a means of "flattening" or "democratizing" other media into a common non-language of zeros and ones, but the vehicle for convergence of irreducible concepts and bodies.

## RECONFIGURING SPACE

It is inherent to M. Chat's status as an art object and cultural intervention to operate on similar principles of convergence as *Chats perchés*:

18. Marie Ottavi, "Le Flashmob fait miauler le parvis de Beaubourg," *Le Parisien* (December 9, 2004): 4.

19. www.artepro.com/actualités/détails/1958480/ (consulted January 7, 2006).

M. Chat is street art, but he is represented by a small Orléans gallery, he is all throughout the web, and we have seen that in December 2004 he was integrated into *the* French National Museum of Modern Art, the Centre Pompidou. Unlike "media convergence" as it is analyzed within industries by communications scholars, M. Chat is relatively removed from commercial motivations—in fact, he does not have much of a "plan" at all—his most important function is simply being. On an Arte "Journal de la culture" broadcast during the day of the tele-vision release, three members of the M. Chat collective—wearing M. Chat masks to preserve their anonymity—were interviewed at the Pompidou Center. Their spokesperson insisted upon the independence of the collective in spite of the current collaboration with Marker and the Centre Pompidou.

> The Cat *is* a collective and it's *staying* a collective. Nobody's gonna come in the Cat collective and say like, yo, I'm the boss, we're doin' this, we're thinkin' that. . . . No way we're gonna be domesticated. [Anyway, we're] not here to say yeah look, we do this, you gotta take it. We put up our thing. People don't like it, they erase it. The ones that stay, it's 'cause people like them and it stays a painting, y'know.[20]

The caution about institutionalization expressed in this interview had not of course prevented M. Chat from embracing the opportunity to pass through the doors opened by Chris Marker's name. As Thoma Vuille of the Galerie Wall stated about the Centre Pompidou events and installation:

> It was national recognition for a generation of urban, post-graffiti artists who, scorned by the cultural elite, pursued by the anti-graffiti police, use the street to express themselves. . . . [They] don't need to speak, the cat already provokes/initiates exchanges between those who create it and those who see it. (Lam, 111)

For M. Chat, the problem of potential co-option and commercializa-tion in fact coalesces around the anonymity of the *Chat* collective. M. Chat's anonymity is in some sense safe—the possibility of (positive) appropriation by ever expanding numbers of street artists would seem to prevent any definitive "selling out" or commercialization. This anonymity is, however, imperfectly preserved as Vuille is commonly regarded as M. Chat's creator amongst M. Chat on-line enthusiasts and,

---

20. M. Chat, interview by Jérôme Cassou, *Arte Journal de la culture* (December 4, 2004) 20:00:50 (1min36).

in a more official register (a footnote to his catalogue essay for Marker's recent exhibition *Staring Back*), Wexner Center Director of Media Arts Bill Horrigan refers to Vuille as "M. Chat's primary begettor."[21] In fact, the Collectif Chat's myspace profile says that Vuille was exposed in March of 2007 "due to an issue with police during painting [sic.] in Orléans."[22]

The problem of institutionalization has of course been a thorny one for the avant-garde in all media and of all time. Recent vocal criticism of British post-graffiti artist Banksy is emblematic of the catch-22 of the street artist who moves off the street and into the gallery. One French reporter outlines M. Chat's problem thus:

> "Monsieur Chat" today inspires dozens of artists (not to mention the copy-cats), and is an object of enthusiasm for more than 500 collectors. This, because he multiplies his media in trying to avoid appropriation—notably mercantile. The copyrighted cat figures, among other places, on a line of t-shirts whose fourth series is distributed by the Galerie Wall. (Lam, 111)

The article continues to explain that, at first, the T-shirts were only distributed to a circle of friends, but—inevitably?—they eventually came to be sold in the gallery. Ironically, M. Chat was designed and came of age in relationship to an Internet culture that promises or at least aspires to escape capitalist control. One blog discussion exchange demonstrates this independent spirit:

> 9. Monday 10 July 2006, 15:40 by jojo
> do you know how to get a m.chat t-shirt? website, shop?

> 10. Sunday 17 September 2006, 23:03, by SkiZz
> Do It Yourself [in English in the original][23]

M. Chat's enthusiasts then, include no-nonsense gatekeepers of anti-establishment resourcefulness of a sort who seem likely to work actively against the kitsch reproduction of artistic images.

In *Chats perchés*, Marker does not miss an opportunity to nod to the capitalist appropriation of engaged, documentary art: Alberto Korda's

21. Chris Marker, *Staring Back*, Wexner Center May 12–August 12, 2007 (Cambridge: MIT Press, 2007), 150.

22. http://profile.myspace.com/index.cfm?fuseaction=user.viewprofile&friend id=27751 *2714* (consulted June 4, 2008).

23. http://www.fubiz.net/blog/index.php?2005/07/28/147-monsieur-chat (consulted January 18, 2007).

Che Guevara photograph appears on a baseball cap at a CGT rally, while a bust of el Che sits in what appears to be the window of a store for musical instruments. There is no missing the reference, as during the CGT rally, the lyrics to the militant music invoke "Che Guevara," and a Latin guitar theme provides the sound for the sequence with the music store. A final reference to Che comes in the sidebar of a *Libération* article that proclaims environmental activist José Bové to be a "modest version of Che Guevara." All of these invocations cause one to rethink the appearance (letter by letter until the end of each word) of the film's title on the opening frames less as an infantile spelling lesson and more as a reconfiguration of C-H-A-TS P-E-R-CHES into Chats per Che, or, Cats for Che.

The independent-mindedness of M. Chat's following has not, however, prevented distributors and institutional events organizers from orchestrating spontaneity such as the flashmob at the Centre Pompidou preview. An image of the Paris audience wearing cat masks has been one of the frequently reproduced press stills (Figure 3). For the May 1 showing at the Tribeca film festival in 2006, First Run/Icarus organized a "March of the Grinning Cats" following the screening. Information about the "Nonsense March" was circulated by email in official press-release format, and was also posted to a site called m-chat.blogspot.com.[24]

On June 10, 2004, Guillaume-en-Egypte/Marker's post to *unregardmoderne* pointed readers to another network that folds bodies and meanings into and out of the so-called virtual and real worlds: the L.A.-based "Freeway blogger," who posts inexpensive home-made signs commenting on matters of current political events on highways, calling it freeway blogging. The Freeway blogger has a website complete with a manifesto explaining his work, instructions on how to be a freeway blogger, and photographs documenting the quite ephemeral interventions. Guillaume's link to www.freewayblogger.com implies support for this "new protest style," one that would perhaps function as a model for his own simultaneous mobilization of web and world spaces in the *Chats* premier six months later. The utopian appeal of the Internet—where the fantasy is of unlimited, dispersed participation in various "communities"—is a logical extension of Marker's continued engagement in leftist politics, even as such communities become indistinguishable from markets.

24. Posted 4/26/06, 1:54 pm (consulted May 1, 2006).

*Figure 3.* Audience at the Centre Pompidou. Courtesy Icarus Films.

M. Chat says that his wings sprouted during the Iraq war—the original artists claim to have had no connection to the cat's appearance on signs during protest rallies. Does M. Chat have political ambitions? Perhaps not on his own. He is, rather, deliberately uncontrolled and out of control, designed to be reproduced by the least of artistic talents, handed over on newsprint to be again reproduced, this time digitally on websites documenting his appearance. His most important potentially political function is to be a nearly empty signifier, allowing anonymous artists of the everyday and their viewers to invest him with their own readings. The proliferation of new media may have increased conduits of disinformation along with those of information (an irony evident in the way Tony Blair and George W. Bush are quoted on weapons of mass destruction in *Chats perchés*). But new media, as a site of interaction between new media and old, the real world and virtual ones, have simultaneously multiplied spaces of creative resistance. Chris Marker, Guillaume-en-Egypte, M. Chat and their various manifestations challenge their audience to continue to define, for themselves, the meaning of engagement, and at least make it seem possible for art to stake out a socially critical and relevant position in the era of global digital culture.

# III. Postcolonial Locations: Francophone Film and Africa

GUY AUSTIN

# "Seeing and listening from the site of trauma": The Algerian War in Contemporary French Cinema

Since 2000 French cinema has engaged repeatedly with a subject that, despite fairly numerous representations on screen over the previous forty years, had always seemed neglected, if not taboo: the Algerian War. This tendency seems particularly visible from 2005 on, whether in documentary form, such as in Alain Tasma's *Nuit noire, 17 octobre 1961* (2006), or, more frequently, in fiction film. Examples of the latter include Philippe Faucon's *La trahison* (*The Betrayal*) (2005), Laurent Herbiet's *Mon colonel* (*The Colonel*) (2006), Florent-Emilio Siri's *L'ennemi intime* (*Intimate Enemies*) (2007) and, at a tangent to the conflict, Michael Haneke's *Caché* (*Hidden*) (2005), or even Rachid Bouchareb's *Indigènes* (*Days of Glory*) (2006). Benjamin Stora has demonstrated that, contrary to widespread perception, the Algerian War was widely represented in French cinema from the sixties on; for example, he identifies 31 French films about the conflict for the period 1962–1982.[1] But despite this cinematographic presence, the war has seemed to remain absent from popular memory in France, so that "the images . . . never really imprinted themselves on the collective consciousness in France."[2] Writing more recently, Stora has stressed the importance of French cinema returning to the places where the conflict happened, and actually filming Algeria rather than a stand-in territory: "One must add that this absence is also an absence of physical locations in French cinema: almost every film about the Algerian war was shot elsewhere,

---

1. See Benjamin Stora, *La gangrène et l'oubli. La mémoire de la guerre d'Algérie* (Paris: La Découverte, 1991), 248.
2. Stora, *Imaginaires de guerre. Algérie, Viet-nam, en France et aux Etats-Unis* (Paris: La Découverte, 1997), 175, italics in original, my translation; all translations are my own unless otherwise indicated.

YFS 115, *New Spaces for French and Francophone Cinema*, ed. James F. Austin,
© 2009 by Yale University.

in Morocco or Tunisia."[3] *La trahison* and *Mon colonel* were in fact both shot in Algeria, although *L'ennemi intime,* a much more action-oriented war movie, was filmed in Morocco. Jean-Pierre Jeancolas contends that in the latter "the location of the war in Algeria is irrelevant; it could just as easily be taking place in Vietnam or Afghanistan."[4] This cannot, however, be said for the other two films—our case studies here—which revisit a specifically Algerian space.

The return to Algeria has a particular resonance for the French imaginary, since it involves a return to the site of trauma. Cathy Caruth has asserted that trauma is "not so much a symptom of the unconscious as a symptom of history." Moreover, trauma has an inherent latency and is therefore "fully evident only in connection with another time and another place."[5] This goes some way to explaining why many French films "about" the Algerian War have tended to concentrate on another time and place (France, after 1962) where the traumatic experience is played out. This is certainly true of French cinema in the years immediately after the ceasefire. The conflict was often left to occupy an off-screen space, so that it remained in a sense unrepresented (indeed, unrepresentable according to Resnais's *Muriel*) and only its impact on French veterans was shown on screen. This tendency has some similarity with the experience of real-life trauma victims, since "the narratives of trauma told by victims and survivors are not simply about facts. They are primarily about the impact of those facts on victims' lives, and about the painful continuities created by violence in their lives."[6] One thinks here of the filmic avatars of the war veteran, exemplified by Popaul in Chabrol's *Le boucher (The Butcher)* (1969). In French cinema of the sixties, then, Algeria remains largely invisible behind the stories of returning soldiers, a traumatizing absence that haunts the French settings of *Ascenseur pour l'échafaud (Elevator to the Gallows)* (Louis Malle, 1957), *Les parapluies de Cherbourg (The Umbrellas of Cherbourg)* (Jacques Demy, 1964), and *Le boucher.* If Malle symbolizes the defeat in Algeria via the figure of "a man trapped

3. Stora, "L'absence d'images déréalise l'Algérie [interview]," *Cahiers du cinéma* Spécial Algérie (February 2003): 9.

4. Jean-Pierre Jeancolas, "French Cinema and the Algerian War: Fifty Years Later," *Cineaste* (Winter 2007): 46.

5. Cathy Caruth, ed., *Trauma: Explorations in Memory* (Baltimore: Johns Hopkins University Press, 1995), 5, 8.

6. E. Ann Kaplan, *Trauma Culture: The Politics of Terror and Loss in Media and Literature* (New Brunswick and London: Rutgers University Press, 2005), 42.

in a lift,"[7] Demy presents a rejected veteran out of place in a changed town, and Chabrol focuses on the eerily silent war memorial and the traumatized butcher's bloody chopping block.[8]

Caruth contends, however, that cinema that most fully realizes the traumatic tends to demonstrate "a seeing and a listening from the site of trauma."[9] For French representations of the Algerian War, this would entail a return to Algeria itself, and in particular to the mountains of Kabylia, the Aurès, and eastern Algeria, where the fighting was heaviest. This is certainly the case in the major documentary *La guerre sans nom* (The nameless war) (Bertrand Tavernier and Patrick Rotman, 1992), with sequences shot in Algeria interspersed with interviews in France and archival footage. Although it is one of the most influential precursors for the current French obsession with remembering Algeria,[10] *La guerre sans nom* persists in the representation of the former colony as an essentially French space.

Naomi Greene wrote in the late nineties about the unfolding of Maurice Papon's trial for war crimes that, "as France confronts the abyss of recent history, the long battle for Vichy memory seems to be drawing to a close."[11] Algeria was on the point of replacing Vichy as a ubiquitous subject of national memory. Within five years or so, the Vichy syndrome identified by Henry Rousso might be said to have given way to an Algeria syndrome. In fact, Rousso has stated that both trends may be described as forms of "hypermnesia," obsessive remembering.[12] A significant early landmark in the Algeria syndrome came on October 18, 1999 when the French parliament officially recognized the "events" in Algeria as a war. A year later, *Le monde* began

---

7. David Nicholls, "Louis Malle's *Ascenseur pour l'échafaud* and the Presence of the Colonial Wars in French Cinema," *French Cultural Studies* 7 (1996): 274.

8. Originally known in French as a *massacre*, the butcher's block gave its name to the mass murders of St. Bartholomew's Day 1572 and to similar events ever since. Chabrol's insistence on shots of Popaul chopping meat suggests he may be aware of the historical, as well as the more visceral and visual, associations at play here.

9. Caruth, "Literature and the enactment of memory," in *Trauma and Visuality in Modernity*, ed. L. Saltzman and E. Rosenberg (Hanover, New Hampshire: Dartmouth College Press, 2006), 214.

10. An obsession that shows no sign of abating. See, for instance, *Le point*, May 22, 2008, with its front-page headline: "Quand l'Algérie était française."

11. Naomi Greene, *Landscapes of Loss: The National Past in Postwar French Cinema* (Princeton, N.J.: Princeton University Press, 1999), 66.

12. See Maryse Bray and Agnes Calatayud, "Remembrance of Things Past: New Perspectives on Films and French Domination in Algeria," *e-France* 1 (2007): 116.

a series of features on the use of torture during the conflict. By the end of 2001, torture in Algeria had been the focus of a study by the historian Raphaëlle Branche and, most sensationally, of the memoirs of General Paul Aussaresses. The war in Iraq (so famously rejected as potential UN policy by Chirac and de Villepin) only intensified the resonance of past atrocities committed in Algeria. A dossier published by *Le monde* in May 2004 entitled "La torture dans la guerre" displayed photos from Abu Ghraib alongside eerily similar images from the Algerian War. The year 2004 also saw the famous screening of *The Battle of Algiers* (Pontecorvo, 1965) at the Pentagon, supposedly in order to show American commanders prosecuting the conflict in Iraq how an occupying power might come to win the battle but lose the war. The film went on to be re-released in France, the US, and the UK. At the same time, French cinema and television were also exploring the Algerian War and related issues. TV movies and mini-series included *L'Algérie des chimères* (François Luciani, 2003) and *Harkis* (Alain Tasma, 2006), while among the television documentaries were André Gazut's *La pacification en Algérie* (Pacification in Algeria) (2002, Arte) and Patrick Rotman's *L'ennemi intime* (2004, France 3). The prolific *pied-noir* director Alexandre Arcady even made a musical about the end of the war, *Les enfants du soleil* (Children of the sun) (2004). Meanwhile, the French and Algerian governments had declared 2003 "the year of Algeria" with cultural celebrations, festivals, and screenings throughout France, plus new French investment for an Algerian film industry crippled by the civil war of the nineties. Conceptually and intellectually, the inter-relation of France and Algeria was being reconsidered, too. In 2004 Paul Silverstein asserted that the two countries had become a "transpolitical" space,[13] and a year later—partly in response to the controversial fourth clause of the law of 23 February 2005, with its call for the teaching of France's "positive" role in the colonies—a group of French sociologists and cultural historians published *La fracture coloniale,* a seminal study of how France was now a postcolonial society dealing with the aftermath of empire.[14]

The films under discussion thus belong to a particularly focused phenomenon of cultural memory. A more neglected factor in French

13. See Charles Forsdick, "Colonial History, Postcolonial Memory: Contemporary Perspectives," *Francophone Postcolonial Studies* 5/2 (2007): 111.
14. Pascal Blanchard, Nicolas Bancel, and Sandrine Lemaire, ed., *La fracture coloniale. La société française au prisme de l'héritage colonial* (Paris: La Découverte, 2005).

representations of Algeria in recent years is the civil war between Islamist groups and the Algerian government that followed the suspension of the 1992 elections and the declaration of a state of emergency. In the decade that followed, up to 200,000 were killed. With its catalogue of terror and counter-terror, torture and trauma, this conflict was viewed by many in France as a repeat of the "events" of 1954–62, and hence as a "second" Algerian War. In 1997 Pierre Bourdieu declared, "it seems that the Algerian War is being replayed . . with a repetition of the same phobias, the same barbaric reflexes, the same brutal reactions of military savagery."[15] Stora has identified this tendency as feeding the revival of French interest in the Algerian War, but has also warned against the simplifications it entails: "It's probably via the current Algerian tragedy that the memory of the first Algerian War has made a comeback in France. . . . Everything is happening as if Algerian history stopped in 1962 . . . and then started up again in 1992, once more marked by violence."[16]

The colonial project in Algeria clearly demarcated spaces assigned to the colonizers and the colonized, in order that the new territory be brought under scrutiny and control. According to Frantz Fanon, "colonization is a success when all this indocile nature has finally been tamed. Railways across the bush, the draining of swamps and a native population which is non-existent politically and economically are in fact one and the same thing." The result was a "world divided into compartments, a motionless, Manichaeistic world."[17] Bourdieu also reminds us that "space is one of the sites where power is asserted and exercised . . . as symbolic violence that goes unperceived as violence."[18] This symbolic violence was doubled in France's occupation of Algeria by actual violence, but the importance of space within social power structures—of which the colony is but an extreme example—remains. Bourdieu continues: "*displacements and body movements* [are] organized by these social structures turned spatial structures and thereby

15. Pierre Bourdieu, "Dévoiler et divulguer le refoulé," in *Algérie—France—Islam,* ed. J. Jurt (Paris: L'Harmattan, 1997), 24.

16. Stora, "L'Algérie d'une guerre à l'autre," in *Apprendre et enseigner la guerre d'Algérie et le Maghreb contemporain,* ed. D. Borne, J-L. Nembrini, and J-P. Rioux (Versailles: Ministére de l'Éducation nationale, 2002), 57–58.

17. Frantz Fanon, *The Wretched of the Earth,* trans. Constance Farrington (London: Penguin Books, 1967), 201, 41.

18. Bourdieu, *The Weight of the World: Social Suffering in Contemporary Society,* trans. Priscilla Parkhurst Ferguson et al (Cambridge, UK: Polity Press, 1999), 25.

*naturalized.* They organize and designate as ascent or descent . . . , entry . . or exit . . what is in fact closeness to or distance from a central, valued site."[19] In the recent films of Michael Haneke and Philippe Faucon these spatial arrangements (margins and center, in and out) are mirrored in cinema (framing, composition) in order to make visible divisions that risk becoming "natural" and hence invisible. In both cases the fear and control of the ethnic other is expressed spatially, and in similar terms, if in distinct settings.

Haneke's *Caché* contrasts the bourgeois Parisian home and workplace of Georges with the tiny flat in the *banlieue* inhabited by Majid. The symbolic journey that separates margin and center is reminiscent of that undertaken by the disaffected *banlieusards* in *La haine* (*Hate*) (Mathieu Kassovitz, 1995). Here the trip is undertaken first by Georges —traveling to a site of social suffering he cannot understand—and then by Majid's son in his visit to George's office. While the housing project where Majid lives may be construed as "la banlieue comme théâtre colonial" [the *banlieue* as colonial space],[20] Georges's work space and domestic space (in both cases shielded by numerous doors and antechambers, and placed above street level) reflect the security and paranoia of the "central, valued site." The infraction of Majid's son into the office building is perceived by Georges as a threat since, despite the civility of the former's language, his very presence here transgresses those social and spatial structures that delimit what Bourdieu calls "displacements and body movements." Put simply, Majid's son is here out of place and his presence reveals the symbolic violence that keeps him out of this privileged site.

If the "central, valued site" in *Caché* is Georges's home and workplace, in Faucon's *La trahison,* set in south-eastern Algeria in 1960, it is the army camp. Outside this camp are to be found the displaced Algerian women and children of the area, often filmed through the wire that separates the two spaces, in an echo of the images that dominate the final scenes of the Algerian classic *Le vent des Aurès* (*The Winds of the Aures*) (Mohamed Lakhdar Hamina, 1966). Where Lakhdar Hamina shoots the French camp from outside the wire, giving the point of view of the mother looking in, Faucon shoots the village and the terrain beyond it from inside the wire, from the soldiers' perspective. It is the divisions within the camp, though, that are Faucon's key concern, cen-

19. Bourdieu, *The Weight of the World,* 126, italics in original.
20. See Blanchard, Bancel and Lemaire, *La fracture coloniale,* 209.

tered as in *Caché* on suspicion of the ethnic other. In this case, these fears concern the four Muslim soldiers in the platoon commanded by Lieutenant Roque (Vincent Martinez). In the compartmentalized world of the colony, their place is not fixed. Already separated from their comrades by their religion and their Algerian origins, the four come under increasing scrutiny after a notebook is discovered on an FLN fighter detailing a plot to kill Roque and turn the camp over to the FLN. Suspicion falls above all on the leader of the four, Taieb (Ahmed Berrhama), who works closely with the lieutenant, as his interpreter.

Just like Majid's son in *Caché*, Taieb is civil, taciturn, and at moments inscrutable, the lack of dialogue and cryptic facial close-ups adding to the tension and uncertainty around his intentions. Moreover, identity is in flux and betrayal omnipresent in *La trahison*, with evidence of treachery and desertion and rumors of secret negotiations between the French and the FLN. It is in this destabilized environment that Roque and his men attempt to ensure the policing of colonial space (driving villagers from their homes, taking a census of civilians and maintaining surveillance of their movements) while the position of the four Muslims in the platoon becomes increasingly ambiguous. The betrayal of the title refers not just to the suspected plot against Roque on their part but also to France's perceived exploitation of these men and their potential abandonment if the war is to be lost (a parallel with the actual fate of the *harkis* in 1962). As Jean-Michel Frodon notes, Faucon expresses the abstract questions regarding the four men—their position, their loyalty, their identity—in spatial terms.[21] Roque and his sergeant take turns on sentry duty to watch Taieb's group as they break their fast during Ramadan. The sergeant's subsequent checks on the Algerian villagers (counting occupants of houses, searching for weapons) reinforce the fact that the Muslim soldiers are being monitored in a similar way. Repeated compositions show all four of them together in the frame, with none of their "français de souche" (pure French) comrades in view. The sense of isolation here, and of having no way out of the frame, is reiterated by the film's conclusion: Taieb and the others are enticed one by one into the back of a truck, an enclosed space where they are handcuffed and driven off to be executed. In one of the very few instances of explanatory dialogue, Roque comments: "They've been caught in a trap, in a situation with no way out."

21. Jean-Michel Frodon, "Ce qui bouge dans le creux de l'histoire," *Cahiers du cinéma* (January 2006): 25–26.

While *La trahison* is filmed with an immediacy, a Bressonian simplicity, and a lack of back-story that seem to place historical trauma in a present tense, even in a documentary style,[22] *Mon colonel* presents a much more layered narrative, dependent on a repeated flashback structure inherited from the thriller genre. Flashbacks have been associated with the symptoms of trauma, in fragmentary and hallucinatory form.[23] According to Caruth, repetition and belatedness also structure traumatic experience: "The event is not assimilated or experienced fully at the time, but only belatedly, in its repeated possession of the one who experiences it."[24] This is evidently the case, for example, in the representation of trauma in *Caché*, where the disruptive arrival of the mysterious video cassettes and drawings call forth a series of sudden, jarring, and disturbing flashbacks in the mind of Georges, the protagonist haunted by unwelcome memories and fantasies of 1961. Although the narrative form of *Mon colonel* is similarly constructed via a series of mysterious parcels that entail repeated flashbacks to the war (here, Algeria in 1956 summoned up by excerpts from Lieutenant Rossi's diary sent to the police by an anonymous killer), the effect is much less disruptive. Where Haneke presents cryptic, nightmarish flashes of traumatized memory, in *Mon colonel* we have a much more conventional, smooth stream of memories, each extensive and chronologically ordered, shown in black and white, mediated by the words of the diary in voice-over, and punctuated regularly by cut-aways to the reader of the diary, the present-day army investigator, Lieutenant Galois (Cécile de France). Here, then, form does not mirror traumatic content. The film does, however, engage with the spaces of trauma in a deliberate and expressive manner.

The opening flashback of *Mon colonel* to 1956 is introduced by the narrative voice-over "And so here I am in Algeria." Rossi (Robinson Stevenin) is shown seated in a jeep being driven through a combat-scarred landscape to his posting at Saint Arnaud. The town is presented as a contested space (via the defiant sign identifying it as a "French city") and will function as such throughout the film, as the French army and the FLN struggle to control its inhabitants. Leading the French garrison is Colonel Duplan (Olivier Gourmet), the victim of a murder in

22. See Frodon, 25.
23. See Kaplan, *Trauma Culture: The Politics of Terror and Loss in Media and Literature*, 69.
24. Caruth, ed., *Trauma: Explorations in Memory*, 4–5.

present-day France, but here the author of repeated strategies designed to display French military control of public space and hence, metonymically, of Algeria itself. Colonel Duplan's picnic, organized to impress upon the local Senator how the surrounding region is under French military control, sees Rossi again seated in a jeep heading through a "dissident landscape," that is to say, a space that facilitates "resistance to central authority" and that has functioned as such throughout Algerian history.[25] In this case, the little French convoy drives through a deep ravine between sheer cliffs, and Rossi's sense of vulnerability is acute. However, as in *La guerre sans nom*, the threat posed to the French army by the alien landscape of Algeria and its (hidden) inhabitants is neutralized by means of the soundtrack. In Tavernier and Rotman's documentary, this is achieved by the use of popular French songs over images of a deserted Algerian landscape. A remarkably similar moment is presented in *Mon colonel* when the French picnic convoy breaks into song while driving though the ravine. The communal singing (symbolizing a collective identity) and its francophone status (denoting a national identity expressed via the French language and consequently imposed upon the colonies) function in both films to control the disputed territory and to mediate the image track, with its views of the "dissident" Algerian landscape. The French language in the form of song appropriates the space, re-creating "French Algeria." Exactly the same technique is used on the mountainside in *Mon Colonel* when Duplan insists that a helicopter-borne priest say mass in full view of the FLN rebels, to demonstrate that he has taken control of that disputed space. The camera pans slowly from left to right across a vast mountainous landscape (its movement indicative of European ideals about progress) while the priest's words and the communal response are heard occupying that space, claiming it as French.[26]

The urban spaces within Saint Arnaud are policed by Duplan in a manner that recalls in microcosm the tactics shown in Pontecorvo's *Battle of Algiers*. Again it is a question of breaking suspected FLN networks by subdividing the populace into sectors and moving through

25. See Martin Evans and John Phillips, *Algeria: Anger of the Dispossessed* (New Haven and London: Yale University Press, 2007), 25.

26. The left-to-right camera movement here is culturally determined. In recent Algerian cinema the influence of Arabic patterns of reading and writing means that camera movement to express progress is usually from right to left. See, for example, the concluding scenes of *L'arche du désert* (*The Ark of the Desert*) (Mohamed Chouikh, 1997) and *Rachida* (Yamina Bachir-Chouikh, 2002).

each sector by means of information-gathering in the form of first a census, then interrogation, and finally torture. The latter takes place in the private space of the torture cell, but more frequently the film presents public space in the town as the real battleground between the army and the FLN. The town square and the stadium are sites given over to public rituals, which become increasingly violent and interconnected as the film progresses. These public areas are crucial since they are the only shared spaces in occupied Algeria: "the two communities co-exist in public space, but not beyond that."[27] The town square is the site of a grenade attack by the rebels and of a display of Algerian corpses by the French. The stadium is the site of a summary execution by Duplan (which Rossi is unable to watch), while the FLN's response is to attach the dead body of an informer to the very same post used by the French firing squad. In a wider sense, the town also operates as a symbol of the French occupation, as its name makes clear. Historically a site of trauma, Saint Arnaud is named after a conquering soldier of the 1830s, infamous for brutal "pacification" measures and described by Victor Hugo as a jackal. This notorious history, into which Duplan has inscribed himself and against which Rossi attempts to maintain his own integrity, is evoked in one of the messages sent by the colonel's murderer: "Duplan died at Saint Arnaud."

It is notable that *Mon colonel* presents the traumatic experience of the Algerian War from the point of view of the well-intentioned young French soldier (Rossi) who comes across atrocities in which he himself is gradually implicated. In this regard (as with its cinematic form) the film is resolutely conventional. It is also strikingly similar to the recent Hollywood movie *In the Valley of Elah* (Paul Haggis, 2007), which takes a comparable approach to the war in Iraq. *La trahison*, however, although also framed as the story of a young lieutenant in Algeria, manages to move beyond its source text (the novel by war veteran Claude Sales) in order to evoke the alienated position of the ethnic other, albeit still within the French army. As in *Caché*, we see French cinema finally starting to engage with the trauma not just of stock figures such as the white French soldier or the FLN-sympathizing French journalist,[28] but of the ethnic Algerian (Taieb/Majid). In 2003, the so-called

27. Stora, "Interview Benjamin Stora," interview by François Malye, *Le point* 1862 (May 22, 2008): 87.

28. See, for example, the film adaptation of Henri Alleg's *La question* (*The Question*) (Laurent Heynneman, 1977).

year of Algeria, Stora wrote of French and Algerian cinema on the conflict that, "everyone remains locked inside his or her own memory. . . . Everyone is seeking a description of his or her own pain, his or her own experience. There's no way to combine experiences or to share the suffering of the other."[29] In the years since 2003, however, films such as *La trahison* and *Caché* have begun to break down this sense of separate traumas, separate spaces. If their lead is followed, we may in time see French films exploring the trauma of the indigenous Algerian population, crossing into a shared space to end the compartmentalization that has characterized the representation of colonial trauma for so long.

29. Stora, "L'absence d'images déréalise l'Algérie," 77.

## PANIVONG NORINDR

# Incorporating Indigenous Soldiers in the Space of the French Nation: Rachid Bouchareb's *Indigènes*[1]

History is a continuous process of liberation and self-awareness.
—Antonio Gramsci

Praised by critics for its realist depiction of indigenous troops who fought valiantly for the liberation of France during World War II, Rachid Bouchareb's 2006 war film *Indigènes* brought to light a little-known chapter in French history. Millions of French moviegoers learned that over 300,000 men from the Maghreb and West Africa had selflessly gone into battle to rid France of its German occupiers, many sacrificing their lives for a country they did not even know. By the end of the film, viewers also learn that four decades after that war, France had still not fully compensated these men for their service to the French nation.[2] President Jacques Chirac and his wife were so moved by *Indigènes* when they first saw the film at the Fondation Georges Pompidou in early September 2006 that it became the emotional catalyst to real political action. Following Chirac's recommendations, on September 27, 2006, the French government authorized benefits for the native troops equal to those of French veterans.[3]

The fact that a fictional movie influenced French policy in such an

1. I would like to thank Grace An and James Austin for their patience and generosity. I am also indebted to Marina Perez de Mendiola for her lucid critique of this essay.
2. The film ends with these words: "In 1959, a law was passed to freeze the pensions of the *tirailleurs* from former French colonies about to become independent. In 2002, after endless hearings, the Council of State ordered the French government to pay the pensions in full. But successive governments have pushed back this payment."
3. In his coverage of Chirac's decision to compensate colonial veterans, Jean-Dominique Merchet presents a fascinating bar chart that reveals the discrepancies between French and "foreign" veterans: the French vet who served at least 90 days in a combat unit receives a yearly average of 430 euros, whereas the Central Africans receive 170, the

**YFS 115,** *New Spaces for French and Francophone Cinema*, ed. James F. Austin, © 2009 by Yale University.

immediate and direct fashion elicited many dithyrambic commentaries in the press.[4] These laudatory remarks, however, seemed to skirt around much more contentious issues, such as French colonialism and its legacy, or the privileging by the mass media of the story of native soldiers who distinguished themselves in battle (the English title, *Days of Glory*, perfectly captures the problematic tone of the movie). The film failed to spark a much needed public debate about French colonial history and the role these *tirailleurs* (native soldiers) played in liberating France from German occupation during both World Wars and, paradoxically, in enforcing France's imperial rule during the decolonization wars in Indochina and Algeria. I argue that despite its popular success and its unprecedented achievement as a militant film-event that will earn its place in film history, *Indigènes* fails to respond to the urgent need for public debate about French colonial history because it represses a more unpalatable truth that contributed to making France what it is today.

If part of the movie's success can be measured by the way it fulfilled its role as a militant film that demanded urgent action from the government, its enduring legacy may be its ability to transform French public perception by re-inserting these *tirailleurs* into France's collective memory and rewriting these forgotten men into history. To comprehend fully the impact of the film, *Indigènes* should be considered in the context of an acutely intolerant moment in French political discourse. The disgruntled French youth who were born and raised in France to immigrant families living in the *banlieue* (suburb), and who rioted in October and November 2005 after the death of two *banlieue* youth pursued by the French police, were described as *racaille* (riffraff) in the intemperate and inflammatory words used by then Minister of the Interior Nicolas Sarkozy. Given French public resentment toward immigrants, especially those from the Maghreb, Bouchareb's film may be said to provide a welcome and effective corrective. But the way *In-*

---

Algerians 57 euros, and the Cambodians 16 euros. Jean-Dominique Merchet, *Libération* (September 26, 2006).

4. Much has been made about the positive impact of the film. Most commentators remark that Bouchareb's film has succeeded in changing French law: "The measure to 'unfreeze' the pay will affect some 80,000 veterans who live, among others, in the former French colonies of black Africa and the Maghreb. At the Cabinet meeting, the French President, Jacques Chirac commented, with emotion, on this measure: 'France fulfills today an act of justice and recognition toward all those from our former French [colonial] empire who fought under our flag.'" M. El Atouabi, *Maroc Hebdo International* (September 29–October 5, 2006). All translations are my own.

*digènes* accomplishes this formidable task is extremely problematic because it reinforces the stereotypical image of the good *indigènes*[5] (natives), loyal and self-sacrificing, and potentially ideal candidates for a full and uncomplicated assimilation into French society. The *indigènes*—and it is always the alien *men*, the *étrangers* and not the *étrangères* (who, as women, are more readily assimilated because of their status as the exotic fiancées, concubines, or wives of Frenchmen)—must show their credentials and prove their worthiness of, and full commitment to, being full-fledged citizens of the French nation. But even being conscripted in the French military and dying for the French nation do not necessarily advance the cause of these men, since they will not be regarded as "equals" in the eyes of French law. And Bouchareb promotes such a reductive view of assimilation *à la française*. He does not develop the character of native solder Abdelkader, for example, the only main figure who begins to question French military authority and unfair practices. (In many interviews, Bouchareb states that Abdelkader is modeled very loosely after the Algerian historical figure Ahmed Ben Bella, who served on the side of the French during World War II, but who becomes one of the FLN leaders during the Algerian War.)

Such a conciliatory nod, even if it proved to be an effective tactic in securing an official gesture of recognition, demonstrates how far France still needs to travel when it comes to reassessing its colonial history. By embracing such a conservative Republican ideal of assimilation for the descendants of these heroic *tirailleurs*, Bouchareb perpetuates the entrenched French belief of assimilation through *reconnaissance* (recognition) that unwittingly does more harm than good to the cause of the indigenous subject or "immigrant" who must first be "recognized" in order to exist from the French public's standpoint. This logic of recognition—in which the glorious service provided by the *indigènes* earns them acknowledgment as heroes, unsung, perhaps, but heroes nevertheless—masks a real need for an in-depth understanding of the legacy of colonialism in the building of the French nation. So rather than *reconnaissance*, or recognition, for services rendered or exceptional contributions in areas such as the armed forces, the film's objective could have been more ambitious by focusing on the much more dense and problematic concept of *connaissance:* knowledge of the his-

5. Bouchareb's "tirailleurs indigènes" seem to be the contemporary tragic version of the *Y-a-bon* figure marketed by the French breakfast chocolate maker during World War I.

tory that binds France to its colonies, including, of course, the role of the *indigènes* in world conflicts and wars of decolonization.

One aim of this essay is to analyze the complex strategies of cultural identification and discursive address mobilized by the filmmaker, both in the film and the *hors-champ* (outside the film, in the off-screen space) in order to incorporate these "natives" into the space of the nation and integrate them in the French imaginary. I contend that Bouchareb's film constructs a problematic space of identification and recognition that borrows much of its force from Hollywood narrative cinema and relies on the most indulgent and manipulative tricks of film technique, such as battle scenes that use special effects and pyrotechnics to suture the viewers to the image and elicit their sympathy, rather than exposing the process by which the French nation has made forgetting possible. These men, I argue, are reinserted in the space of a nationalist pedagogy that privileges the Republican ideal of *intégration* (assimilation) over a process of *connaissance* (knowledge). By examining the inscription of these subjects within a nationalist discourse, one finds that *Indigènes* unwittingly homogenizes the experience of these men, erases cultural difference, and, more problematically, elides colonial history by failing to narrate the story of French colonial repression in the Maghreb during World War II—in May 1944 in the Riff for instance. It thus offers yet another simplified account of the incorporation of native troops in the French war effort.

Unlike Frantz Fanon in *Les damnés de la terre* (1961) or Ousmane Sembène in *Camp de Thiaroye* (1987), who both concentrate on "unruly natives," Bouchareb focuses on the loyal Maghreb soldiers who fought for France without considering the consequences of French colonial violence in the Maghreb and other occupied territories. Very timidly, he asks the viewer to reflect on the cost of this loyalty in a scene when surviving members of the platoon spot the propaganda leaflets dropped by the Germans that ask these Maghrebi solders why they are still fighting on the side of the French, their oppressor. When pressed by Sergeant Martinez, the commanding NCO, to respond, Abdelkader immediately pledges his loyal devotion to the French nation.

Bouchareb wanted to share the unknown story of these men with his countrymen and the rest of the world. To narrate their stories, he and his collaborators culled French archives to find traces of their presence on the battlefields of European war. In interviews, the filmmaker often mentions the difficulty of finding material during the year spent researching the story, and the two and a half years it took to write the screenplay. Many of the original materials were found scattered in French archives: army reports of letters censoring amorous relations between these native men and French women, photographs of native soldiers wearing *sandalettes* instead of boots in the bitter cold of a winter campaign, or of men who were known to have been ordered to engage in deadly assaults against heavily fortified enemy positions, so that the French artillery and air force could determine their exact coordinates and destroy these well-defended strategic positions. All of these micro-narratives and "historical" details would be woven into Bouchareb's screenplay, shaping the fictional narrative and providing the historical dimension or reality effect of the film. Bouchareb and Olivier Lorelle, his co-screenwriter, also used the oral testimonies of veterans, not only form the Maghreb, but also from West Africa and Indochina, to reconstruct the history of their engagement and pull these figures out of the margins and footnotes of French history books. Bouchareb acknowledged the challenge of such an assignment: "We conducted extensive research in archives. The fact is that we found very few images."[6] His movie, then, can be said to supplement the official French depiction of France's liberation during World War II, which is always represented as an almost exclusively Franco-French affair, as the famous photograph of the liberation of Paris after the entry of the French 2nd Armored Division signifies so well, erasing the "foreign contingents," the *indigènes* of the colonial troops.

According to the film critic Dider Peron (*Libération*, September 25, 2006), "For the first time, a movie makes use of all the resources of popular entertainment for a historical reconstruction that also casts A-list actors in order to correct the mutilated vision of a popular audience that continues to misjudge the period, a vision systematically 'whitened' to the detriment of the goums, Maghrebi spahis, and other Senegalese *tirailleurs.*" Bouchareb's film indeed shows men in action, fighting in a war in which they had no real stakes. It perhaps even succeeded in enlightening a wide audience in spectacular fashion. It is, however, legitimate to point out the high cost of the vulgarization of history, "trivialized" by the *grand spectacle* ethos and exacerbated by the filmic genre adopted by the filmmaker.

---

6. Rachid Bouchareb, "'L'affirmation de notre identité française,'" interview by Ange-Dominique Bouzet, *Libération* (September 25, 2006).

## ON GRAND NARRATIVE AND FILMIC STRUCTURE, AND THE PROBLEMATIC NARRATIVIZATION OF HISTORY

The choices of the war film genre and the grand historical narrative were made in part because the director believed that only an ambitious, spectacular big-budget film would do justice to the story of these men. He enrolled the help of very famous beur actors like Jamel Debbouze, who co-starred in the film and was one of its producers. The importance of casting a star of such stature is not insignificant since it was largely because of Debbouze that the Moroccan government provided much of the logistical support for the costly war reenactments. More than 500 Moroccan army troops were used as extras for the elaborate battle scenes. The film moreover, is co-produced, backed financially by Morocco as well as by France and Belgium, and financed to the tune of 14.48 million euros. In comparison, the same year, Bruno Dumont's *Flandres* cost only 2.12 million, Abdellatif Kechiche's *La graine et le mulet*, 6.14 million, and Pascale Ferran's *Lady Chatterley*, 2.33 million.

But how is the film historically grounded? Bouchareb uses black and white newsreel footage in the opening credit sequence in an attempt to ground it in the real and make it appear as historically driven narrative. Bouchareb explains his motivations in these terms:

> Opening with these archival black and white images of the French colonial empire puts the audience in conditions very similar to those of the events documented at the time. We used historical information as a foundation. I then used . . . images in black and white from time to time to open different scenes, to serve as a reminder of the opening images. And that gives the film its veracity. As for the visual aspects, I wanted a khaki look, the color of military uniforms, neither shiny nor aesthetic and it wasn't always easy to get that shade right.[7]

The "historical information" to be gleaned from these rapidly passing moving images can hardly be described as foundational. The numerous views that fill the movie screen constitute an impressionistic tapestry of the Maghreb, reminiscent of propaganda exhibited to elicit Metropolitan support for France's colonial project. The initial newsreel is of four Maghrebi men sowing a field, with shots of a horse-drawn plow, tractors, and other mechanized farm equipment; in a second small

---

7. Bouchareb, interview by Fabien Lemercier, *CineEuropa* (September 20, 2006).

screen that appears along with the newsreel, an Algerian woman can be seen going to the market; a third view shows a man parading on horse-back at an unidentified ceremony; in a fourth, a native woman is seen dancing. In all, at least thirteen small screens vie for the viewer's attention. Whether one notices the Arab sultan parading on his white horse, the workers laboring with their shovels on a road, the busy docks and the steam-ships being loaded, native men cavorting, a caravan of camels, and even the Boulangerie du Maréchal Pétain, is not vital for comprehending the rest of Bouchareb's film; all this seems, at best, a haphazard effort. In fact, none of these views can be easily identified, and it is only with repeated viewing that one can even attempt a superficial decoding of these images. Even more dubious is the claim that these black and white archival images document real events at a particular time in history. It is to accept too readily that cinema is a transparent medium that records reality faithfully, without any consideration of cinematic mediation.

In fact, these "newsreels" are of the *scènes et types* (scenes and types) genre that were used so effectively by many colonial governor-generals throughout the French colonial empire to shore up France's civilizing mission. They showcase the French *mise-en-valeur* (development) of these unexploited "barren lands," reinforcing the colonial stereotypes disseminated by earlier technologies, such as the chromolithograph, photography, and the postcard. The assumed but tenuous "veracity" of the credit sequence, then, accompanied by an original score by the most famous Algerian raï singer, Khaled, and by composer Armand Amar, and sung hauntingly by the former, simply fails to convey the thick history of the colonial troops' engagement in General de Gaulle's French Free Forces.

In Bouchareb's defense, *Indigènes* is a narrative film and not a documentary, as he readily admits. This strategic choice will determine, as we will see below, the aesthetic look of the film and permits the easy classification of *Indigènes* in the war genre. The recognition of their sacrifice, the director hopes, will retroactively bestow on these men a heroic genealogy of their presence on French soil, and provide a valiant lineage to their descendants in our time. This is to attribute to cinema a transformative power, to endow it with a positive force capable of changing the self-image of a million young Beurs and immigrants, and of altering the public perception of these men and women. Does cinema, in the twenty-first century, have such a power or mandate to edify?

Both the popular success and (in the eyes of this critic) failure of

Bouchareb's film can be attributed to the director's impressionistic understanding of history, deployed in the service of a cinematographic writing that as much reifies and memorializes as it illuminates a veiled corner of French history. On the positive side, one can certainly appreciate a narration told from the point of view of four Maghrebi soldiers who are no longer portrayed as violent shadowy figures, as was the case in Vittorio de Sica's *La Ciociara* (1960), but rather as full-fledged subjects who, similarly, are not anonymous and who have names: Abdelkader (played by Sami Bouajila), Saïd Otmari (Jamel Debbouze), Yassir (Samy Naceri), and Messaoud Souni (Roschdy Zem). This shift in perspective allows the filmmaker to tell a different story about these men whose valor in battle was acknowledged but not officially recognized (they were promoted as non-commissioned officers less frequently than French soldiers). They were deprived of other privileges enjoyed by their French counterparts, such as the authorization to go on leave after months fighting in bloody battles, or the same quality of food. In one memorable sequence, the native troops are defiant because the French cooks refuse to give them fresh tomatoes, reserved for French soldiers. Bouchareb told journalist Ange-Dominique Bouzet: "The sequence relating to the fresh tomatoes reserved exclusively for the 'French' canteen is also a truly lived anecdote." (Bouchareb, "'L'affirmation de notre identité française'").

In spite of these brilliant moments, the screenplay uses conventional "découpage," following the men's "enrollment" in Algeria and Morocco, and then their perfunctory training in Morocco and Sétif in 1943, before their first engagement in Italy in 1944. The training sequence is a montage of shots, depicting men marching in full gear ("like mules," as one soldier put it), spirit boosting talk by French army officers who explain the rules of engagement ("We permit raids in enemy territory for food, but hands off the women or you'll be shot. In France, no raids at all. We show discipline! It's our home, our motherland"), and classroom instructions for the French and the few natives who can read and write. It ends with a rather predictable scene of "incorporation" through the performance of the famous colonial army song, "C'est nous les Africains,"[8] sung in unison by the new recruits of the Armée d'Afrique, with words and image in seemingly perfect harmony with the film's ethos:

8. Dominique Lormier, *C'est nous les Africains: L'épopée de l'armée d'Afrique 1940–1945* (Paris: Calmann-Lévy, 2006).

We are the Africans
Who come from afar
We come from the colonies
To save the fatherland
We have left everything
Parents, gourbis, homes
And we have at heart
An invincible ardor
Because we want to carry high and proud
The cherished flag of sweet France
And if someone were to try to take it away
We would be ready to be killed for it
Beat the drums, for our lovers,
For our country, for our homeland
To die afar
We are the Africans.

Indeed, these selfless men have come from the colonies to help save the French nation and liberate it from its oppressors. If we are to believe the lyrics, they are also willing to sacrifice themselves and die so that "the cherished flag of sweet France" can be raised "high and proud." In the last image of this sequence, the French flag flutters high in the luminous blue sky of North Africa. The rest of the film seems to materialize the lyrics of "coming from afar to die." Bouchareb follows the indigenous members of the platoon led by Sergeant Martinez and Corporal Abdelkader in the campaigns of Italy, Provence, the Rhone Valley, and ending in the Vosges in November 1944. Of course, they distinguish themselves on these battlefields and consolidate their reputation as soldiers loyal to France, despite the bitterly unsettling discriminatory practices mentioned above.

In the penultimate sequence, when all but one of the native soldiers in the platoon are killed while fighting a German company in the defense of an Alsatian village *à la Saving Private Ryan*, Abdelkader, the sole survivor, wanders out of the village alone, having just been ordered to join another platoon. He sees an army cameraman filming a group of village women surrounded by only recently arrived French soldiers. "Look over here," the cameraman tells them as he films them close up, and then asks them to pose and smile for the camera. More problematically, he utters the following words: "French soldiers free Alsace!" under Abdelkader's incredulous gaze. Only the villagers, the sole witnesses to his feat of arms, applaud him discreetly to express their gratitude.

This scene crystallizes the problems Bouchareb encountered in the archive. As suggested earlier, when he searched for traces these men had left in official army records, he found very few images of them. This sequence attempts to provide an explanation for the failure to find photographic or moving images of these indigenous troops who were rarely the privileged subjects of the French army propaganda apparatus. But if Bouchareb succeeded in conveying the dearth of moving images through these fleeting shots recorded by the French cameraman, the statement "French soldiers free Alsace!" produces the unfortunate effect of returning the viewer to a didactic history lesson. We have just witnessed the heroic actions of native troops who died tragically defending this unnamed Alsatian village. There was no compelling reason to underscore the irony of the situation any further for a now informed public.

Narrating the captivating story of these native troops may have proved to be as difficult a task as using "real" history as the foundation for his screenplay. In fact, Bouchareb's biggest blunder occurs in the very opening sequence of the movie. Just after the black and white fade to the color panoramic shot of a small village in "Algeria 1943," as the caption informs the viewer, a man's voice, speaking in Arabic, is heard urging his compatriots to enlist; the subtitle reads: "We must rid France of the German occupation! Come along! Come with me." We see an Arab man, walking through a village and crying, "We must wash the French flag with our blood!" He tells the villagers, "Come with me! Let's have the men out! We must liberate France. Liberate her! We must save France from this situation. Come on!" Young Arab men, among them Saïd, are portrayed as docile "volunteers" who follow, on their own accord, the Arab recruiter to the French army trucks awaiting them.

If Western film critics have paid little attention to this opening sequence, its veracity has been bitterly debated and contested in Algeria, as well as discussed by a historian such as Benjamin Stora who points to this very problematic section of the movie (Le monde, September 26, 2006):

> First, the question of enlistment. One sees a noteworthy native who calls on men in their villages to convince them to go rescue France. And then, the volunteers board trucks with enthusiasm. It did not happen like that everywhere. Admittedly, there is, in the Maghreb, a tradition of enlisting in the Army of Africa as a means for social advancement and to provide food for one's family. By enlisting in the army, one ob-

tains benefits, a pension, and the opportunity to learn how to read and write. But there is also a tremendous amount of mistrust, insubordination, and disobedience, particularly among the peasantry. That was the case even before World War I. In 1911, several hundreds families in Tlemcen refused to surrender their sons and fathers to the draft, and preferred to leave Algeria for the Middle East. In 1916, an uprising broke out in the Aurès. . . . Enlistment was often forced.

To suggest that these impoverished men volunteered to serve under the French flag seems disingenuous at best, and a particularly unconvincing way of explaining a lesser known facet of World War II history, and demonstrating the contributions of the indigenous troops to the liberation of France. Of course, this suggestion allowed the filmmaker to introduce one of the main protagonists, the very poor Saïd who leaves home in search of a better life. Should we attribute this "faux pas" to artistic license or simple demagoguery?

I submit that Bouchareb feels the force of two competing and often incompatible visions of history: one that privileges "popular memory" (eyewitness accounts and lived experiences) over the one reconstructed by trained historians who favor the scientific, rational account that suppresses emotional and personal relations as well as sentimentalizing narratives. Bouchareb's primary target audience is certainly not made up of film or cultural critics, historians, and other academics. As a professional screenwriter and filmmaker, Bouchareb instrumentalizes history in order to reach a young, popular audience, one that scorns the documentary genre, and favors well-made action films animated by vibrant pyrotechnics. In *Indigènes*, Bouchareb has certainly indulged them. But, far more interestingly, he has also admitted that the project began as a rather personal quest for self-knowledge and the need to understand his own story:

> My first need was to understand my own history. What did our ancestors, for us children of immigrants, experience under colonization? What role did our grandparents and parents play in the war and in the reconstruction of France? I have cared for and worried about this project for years. I spent a long time investigating and meeting many war veterans. Not only North Africans, but also Asians and [other] Africans. . . . Initially, the screenplay included a black soldier, but it ran over four hours. Be that as it may, I don't consider *Indigènes* to be a communitarian film for the community. Neither I nor the actors! It is a general act of affirmation of our French identity, for all the sons [*fils*] of immigration. (Bouchareb, "'L'affirmation de notre identité française'")

The scope of the original project was therefore both more personal, on the one hand, and broader in its ambition, on the other, since it did not limit itself to the war stories of the soldiers but also included those of sub-Saharan African and Asian veterans. Bouchareb appeared inquisitive about French colonialism, in general, as well as the role immigrants played in France's postwar reconstruction. Nevertheless, he also reveals a rather parochial and static understanding of identity. He wants to dispel any misunderstanding about his film that would mislead some into believing that *Indigènes* is a "communitarian film for the community." On the contrary, he claims, it is a way to affirm "French identity, for all the sons of immigration." There is no doubt that his film will never be criticized or taken to task for its critique of Frenchness. It never offers any substantial or sustained criticism of French colonial policies,[9] except for the unequal pay of colonial veterans. This was not the case with Ousmane Sembène who, in his 1987 fiction film *Camp de Thiaroye,* did not hesitate to portray the murderous violence of the French and their slaughter of the heroic *tirailleurs sénégalais* after they were shipped back in late 1944 and repatriated to the transit Camp of Thiaroye in Senegal, and eventually demobilized and sent back home to their respective countries throughout West Africa. Some of these men had been imprisoned in concentration camps, while others had participated in the Italian and French campaigns. Because these veterans wanted to be paid what was owed to them at the full local exchange rate, they briefly took as hostage the French general assigned to resolve the emerging crisis. In spite of his promise to find a peaceful resolution, the general, after being liberated, orders a motorized army unit to shell the camp and machine-gun the unarmed "mutineers."

Although Bouchareb dealt very briefly with this dark episode in French military history in his animated short, *L'ami Y-A-Bon* (2004; 9 min), *Indigènes* supports a rather reactionary vision of loyalty and cultural integration, one that blindly endorses all the values of Republican France. For example, we learn that Yassir's parents were killed by the occupying colonial army, and yet Yassir and his brother do not hold any grudges against the French since they "volunteer" to join the

---

9. In Bouchareb's film, none of the main characters challenges the colonial situation and the continued presence of France in the Maghreb and sub-Saharan Africa. They have yet to be conscious of their inscription in history and are therefore not yet Gramscian subjects of history.

Armée d'Afrique (admittedly for money so that the younger brother can marry). Also problematic is the fact that *Indigènes* does not even suggest that some of the men who gained wartime experience in these world conflicts would become key figures in later independence efforts and the decolonizing wars against the French.

Instead, Bouchareb prefers a much more conciliatory approach. His film ends with a huge temporal jump. The intertitle reads: Alsace, 60 years later. The scene begins with a panoramic shot of a military cemetery and a field of white crosses, and of course, the French flag. Abdelkader is now an old man searching for the tomb of his fallen comrades. He finds a concrete cross that reveals, in a close-up shot, the presence of "Roger Martinez, Staff Sergeant . . . 7th Regiment of Algerian Tirailleurs. Died for France 1-15-1945" inscribed on a plaque. He then searches for and prays on the tomb of Saïd before returning "home" on public transportation. The audience sees him walking alone, an anonymous and invisible man within a large crowd, unrecognized as a war hero, returning to his substandard room, furnished with only the bare necessities: a single bed, a chair, and a washbasin. He has a broken, pensive air. The last shot of the movie returns to the military cemetery, but this time it is not the usual field of white crosses in the foreground, but the hundreds of Arab steles, with the French Flag once again flowing in the wind. As Bouchareb explained:

> the final scene closes with Muslim steles in military cemeteries of the two world wars, which had never before been shown in cinema. It is this battle that we see today and one in which I tried to participate calmly, that of history, and [of] which history should be the reference for the world. With *Days of Glory,* we tell how more than 300,000 soldiers from the colonies committed themselves to liberate France: no one had ever done that before. (Bouchareb, *CineEuropa*)

In fact, Bouchareb is not the first filmmaker to examine the untold story of these native *tirailleurs.* For the past twenty years, a number of documentary filmmakers and independent film directors have foregrounded the role of these colonial soldiers in the First and Second World Wars, and the Indochinese and Algerian Wars. In his 1985 documentary, *L'histoire oubliée: Soldats noirs* (Forgotten History, Black Soldiers), Eric Deroo focuses on the 40,000 so-called "Senegalese" *tirailleurs,* who in fact came from all the sub-Saharan French colonies and fought for France as early as 1939. Forty-five years after the war, he interviews villagers from the Ardennes who pay homage to their incredible feat of arms and courage, and the veterans themselves, who narrate very simply their *épopée d'anciens combattants* (veterans' epic). *C'est nous les Africains . . . eux aussi ont libéré l'Alsace* (We Are the Africans . . . They Too Liberated Alsace), a documentary by Petra Rosay and Jean-Marie Fawer (1994), traces the "participation of Algerian and Tunisian soldiers" in the liberation of Alsace who decide to settle in Alsace after the war. Their testimonies focus on both their engagement in the French army and their difficult integration in Alsacian society. And Africans have themselves been involved in telling their own story. *Devoir de mémoire* (The Duty to Remember), by Cheick Tidjane Ndiaye, from Senegal, examines the role of Africans in the liberation of France during World War II. Imunga Ivanga, from Gabon, focuses in *Les tirailleurs d'ailleurs* (The Native Troops from Elsewhere) (1996) on his own father, Luc Marc Ivanga, who joined the 15th Regiment of Senegalese Troops, and fought the Nazis from 1939 until 1945. He and three other comrades-in-arms discuss the painful past, and trace their emotional reactions to the war and its aftermath, from *insouciance* to the grim reality of war, and finally, their disillusion after so many promises were not kept. Filmmakers have also sought to evoke the sacrifice of other indigenous troops. Bernard Simon's *Les tirailleurs malgaches* (The Malagasy Colonial Troops) (2003) searches for the Malagasy fighters who fought in the French army from 1939 to 1945, and in Indochina and Algeria as well. He probes such a fundamental question as their status as "volunteers," which Bouchareb simply accepts as truth and historical fact in *Indigènes*. Rather than merely inquiring, moreover, about these soldiers' motivations for fighting or what they have lived through and endured, Simon wonders how many have survived the many wars of the twentieth century and what they have become today. Eric Beauducel, in *Le bataillon des guitaristes* (The Guitarist Batallion) (2004), follows the six hundred volunteers from New Caledonia and French Polynesia who left the Pacific in 1940 to fight in France, and places them beside the African *tirailleurs* in the fight and sacrifice for the liberation of France. And he does not neglect the Indochinese fighters who are the real unknown heroes of the French resistance. Euzhan Palcy's *Parcours de dissidents* (The Dissidents' Journey) (2006) traces the perilous journey from Martinique to France, via Morocco and Italy, taken by the young Antillean men who responded to General de Gaulle's June 18, 1940 appeal to help France fight the Nazis.

Unlike Fanon or Sembène, who focused on the "unruly natives,"

Bouchareb prefers to deal with the loyal *indigène* soldiers who supposedly "volunteered" their service to fight for France. He repeated in countless interviews that these men never regretted their enlistment. Thanks to Cheikh Djemai, and his brilliant *Frantz Fanon: sa vie, son combat, son travail* (Frantz Fanon: His Life, Struggle, and Work) (2004), one can enter as counter-evidence the letters Frantz Fanon wrote to his family from the front, after he had fled Martinique to join the French Free Forces. He complained bitterly about how the French army treated men of color like him as second-class citizens. The army's racist actions led a depressed and suicidal Fanon to volunteer for the most dangerous missions.

As a fiction film about the *tirailleurs*, Bouchareb's film pales in contrast to both Oumarou Ganda's *Cabascabo* and Sembène's classic *Camp de Thiaroye*. And even though the DVD is marketed today as "the true story of the heroes that changed the course of history," it is, as I have suggested above, far from being a "true story." *Indigènes* changed the course of history by providing financial redress to the 56,700 native veterans from more than twenty countries who are still alive today. Yet *Indigènes* will ultimately be remembered as a mediocre war film, in large part because it blindly borrows a Hollywood model, from its narrative structure to its diachronic temporality, that fails to account for the ruptures and discontinuities of history. As Paul Ricoeur had demonstrated in his masterful *L'histoire, la mémoire, l'oubli* (2000), the lure of *reconnaissance* undermines the slow process of achieving real *connaissance*, and leads to forgetting. By not ending his film with the Sétif Massacre of May 1944, or with the emergence of the nationalist movement and rise of FLN leaders like Ahmed Ben Bella, a veteran of the Italian campaign and Monte Cassino, Bouchareb unwittingly reinscribes these men as historical objects in the space of a conservative nationalist pedagogy instead of portraying them as victorious agents of historical change.

## DOMINIC THOMAS

# Africa/France: Contesting Space

The production and distribution of francophone sub-Saharan African films remains inextricably linked to a cultural, economic, political, and social history of interaction between Africa and France. Lines of demarcation between films made in Africa and/or in France have been blurred as a result of a complex network of transversal influences, and ultimately contested in these concrete and imaginative spaces. Since at least the 1970s, African-centered films have evaded simple categorization, and the degree of interpenetration has been reflected in films featuring African populations in Africa, in the diasporic communities of France and Europe, and among ethnic minorities and immigrant populations. In turn, the multiplicity of topographic spaces in which francophone African films have been located announces a significant expansion and decentralization of the parameters of French-language film production, a phenomenon that has been accompanied by a thematic evolution addressing the issues confronting ethnic minority populations. An analysis of recent developments in francophone African diasporic films necessarily engages with the dual components of this equation, namely those elements pertaining to the new spaces in which film production operates *and* the actual evidentiary mode represented by an African presence in these spaces.

An exhaustive account of these circumstances would call for a much longer and sustained analysis than I can attempt here; nevertheless, consideration of a selection of films by Med Hondo (Mauritania), Zeka Laplaine (Democratic Republic of the Congo), Idrissa Ouedraogo (Burkina Faso), and Jean-Marie Teno (Cameroon) can serve to identify some of the ways in which territorial displacement and spatial reconfiguration have been employed to more accurately contextualize the shifting global landscape of African/French postcolonial relations. Pat-

**YFS 115,** *New Spaces for French and Francophone Cinema,* ed. James F. Austin,
© 2009 by Yale University.

terns of immigration and government responses to these have become indissociable from the subjects addressed by African and/or minority filmmakers. These have often coincided with demographic changes and the resulting claims for inclusion and belonging by Africans despite various obstacles. Additionally, francophone film has included production at extra-hexagonal sites within the European Union itself as a consequence of new intra-European funding structures and modifications to regulations concerning population mobility within that geographic zone. These adjustments are historically relatively recent, and have not always been sufficiently anticipated or accounted for by film critics. For example, while acknowledging the vibrancy and "the diversity of movements in African cinema" at the end of the 1980s, Manthia Diawara's prognostic for African cinema remained for the most part very much Africa (as continent) centric.[1] In contrast to Diawara's ideas, not only Africa but both France and Europe now are relevant for African cinema.

A foundational component of French direct rule during the colonial era was provided by the imperative of deploying a civilizing mission with the specific objective of forming French cultural prototypes. Not surprisingly, such a program would have recourse to the multidimensional qualities offered by film as a propagandist mechanism, and the Comité de Propagande Coloniale par le Film was inaugurated as early as 1928. As Peter Bloom has indicated in his book *French Colonial Documentary: Mythologies of Humanitarianism*, "The promotion of colonial educational cinema was auxiliary to a vision of colonial humanism . . . that linked economic development to moral, political, intellectual, educational, and social values."[2] Shortly thereafter, in 1934, the Laval decree was signed into law (named after the French Minister of the Colonies). Its purpose was to "control the content of films that were shot in Africa and to minimize the creative roles played by Africans in the making of films" (Diawara, 22). The colonial authorities were only too aware of the subversive potential of film as a tool for consciousness raising and wasted no time imposing restrictions on autonomous modes of film production. In a somewhat paradoxical manner, these restrictive measures were to play an unexpected role in

1. Manthia Diawara, *African Cinema: Politics and Culture* (Bloomington: Indiana University Press, 1992).

2. Peter Bloom, *French Colonial Documentary: Mythologies of Humanitarianism* (Minneapolis: University of Minnesota Press, 2008), 128.

African film history, since young African filmmakers trained in France were essentially able to bypass these early rules and regulations governing film production and produce films in the Hexagon itself, most notably Paulin S. Vieyra's *Afrique-sur-Seine* in 1955. Such developments and complex reformulations of national and territorial affiliation epitomize the broader sphere of francophone African film production and the resulting negotiation that has taken place between African and diasporic films.

Similar conditions have been in evidence in a transcolonial context where we have witnessed the transfer of colonial realities to the postcolonial era. The Écrans du Sud, for example, a funding mechanism implemented following the 1991 Sommet de la Francophonie, had the objective of giving "southern-hemisphere filmmakers an instrument that was more independent, less bound up with the state and hence not so dependent on the political developments which might possibly constrain the various government departments."[3] However, one of the problems with the funding structure of the Écrans du Sud was its insistence, irrespective of a director's residency, that "a film must be made in Africa" (Barlet, 269). Effectively, colonial structures of control were reversed in this instance, as the French authorities have continued to attempt to exercise control over both the production and content of African films, replacing the initial concern with anticolonial oppositional with an updated version that reveals an apprehension of denunciations of the contemporary treatment and social status of postcolonial African minorities in France itself. For Med Hondo, though, "difficulties in finding backing for his films are in no way unique, but they illustrate a state of affairs that the Mauritanian filmmaker has been denouncing repeatedly—the colonization of Black Africa by Western cinema."[4]

Any treatment of ethnicity and race in France is inevitably infused with broader questions pertaining to Republican principles of citizenship, and comparative analysis with other European countries reveals the particularity of these circumstances. As Carrie Tarr has indicated:

> there is no structural support for minority filmmakers within the French film industry and TV industry comparable to the BFI [British

---

3. Olivier Barlet, *African Cinemas: Decolonizing the Gaze*, trans. Chris Turner (London and New York: Zed Books, 2000), 268–69.

4. Madeleine Cottenet-Hage, "Decolonizing Images: *Soleil O* and the Cinema of Med Hondo," in *Cinema, Colonialism, Postcolonialism: Perspectives from the French and Francophone Worlds*, ed. Dina Sherzer (University of Texas Press, Austin, Texas, 1996), 175.

Film Institute] and Channel Four in Britain. As a consequence, film-makers from France's former colonies, many of whom have studied and/or worked in France, or live in France on a more or less permanent basis . . . find themselves making films that primarily address a French/European art-house audience.[5]

Official French policy in the cultural domain reflects adherence to those principles of Republican citizenship that concern undifferentiated subjects. As Melissa Thackway has argued, "French critics and audiences, conditioned by a tradition of 'assimilationist' policies and an official anathema to the existence of communities, still have difficulty in accepting a critical African gaze in their own country."[6] There remains much confusion around the attempt to categorize these films, "whether such works are better seen as part of a 'Black French,' rather than an 'African cinema'" (Thackway, *Africa*, 145), questions that were answered decades ago across the Channel where the coordinates of a multicultural infrastructure had been carefully delineated. Nevertheless, "how the European films made by Francophone African directors are received in France and what this says about the position they occupy in the French cinematographic landscape" (Thackway, *Africa*, 145) can contribute not only to a more nuanced understanding of the general context but also to the manner in which obstacles and prohibitions have not succeeded in preventing the emergence of committed films that replicate the "cultural nomadism of African filmmakers."[7] The *nomadism* or mobility of African filmmakers relates both to the funding infrastructure elaborated earlier that necessitates adaptability and flexibility, and to displacement patterns that are intrinsic to those global historical experiences that in turn have provided the material for films made in Africa or in diasporic contexts.

A cursory overview of films made by Africans in France reveals a corpus that includes such filmmakers as Paulin S. Vieyra (*Afrique-sur-Seine*, 1955), Inoussa Ousseini (*Paris c'est joli*, 1974), and Ben D. Beye (*Les princes noirs de Saint-Germain-des-Prés*, 1975). These films were

5. Carrie Tarr, "French Cinema and Post-Colonial Minorities," in *Post-Colonial Cultures in France*, ed. Alec G. Hargreaves and Mark McKinney (London: Routledge, 1997), 60. Channel 4 is a British commercial television broadcaster launched in the early 1980s and reputed for its support of independent and innovative programming.

6. Melissa Thackway, *Africa Shoots Back: Alternative Perspectives in Sub-Saharan African Film* (Bloomington: Indiana University Press, 2003), 1.

7. Melissa Thackway, "Images d'immigrés," *Cinémas africains, une oasis dans le désert*, ed. Samuel Lelièvre, *CinémAction* 106 (2003): 50.

innovative and have contributed to the expansion of the parameters of *both* African *and* French filmography. Thematically, these films augment a long list of films that have addressed the living conditions of ethnic minorities and immigrants, as well as "their asymmetrical relationships with French individuals, their negative interactions with French authorities, and the poverty, racism, and unemployment that plague the young people."[8] "The emergence of a cinema that has begun to portray the real rooting of the African community in France" (Thackway, *Africa,* 145) has been important to the process of diversifying the ways in which this population is represented.

Whereas French films have endeavored to address the presence of immigrant populations, the primary concern has been either with the integrational obstacles confronting these groups or with the alleged problems they present to the assimilationist ideals of the French Republic. The degree to which these new films have challenged the cultural and political landscape of the Hexagon and accordingly generated contestation over space and discourse are exemplified in Olivier Barlet's suggestive question, "Are the new films from Africa really African?"[9] Barlet delineates a chronology that runs from early debates around the question of multiculturalism during the 1980s through the issues of the 1990s that included both urban riots and discussions over the appropriate treatment of undocumented/illegal migrant subjects, collectively ascribed the label *sans-papiers* (illegal/undocumented subjects). It is to this latter category, namely the *sans-papiers,* that I now turn our attention.

The social and political context cannot be decoupled from the analysis of these films, since the concern with the demographic make-up of the European Union has in numerous ways contributed to the increased focus on illegal and/or undocumented subjects circulating within "Fortress Europe." Not surprisingly, these issues have disproportionately impacted minority populations and played a central role in the amplification of francophone film production away from a uniquely Hexagon-centric model. Certain films, set in multiple locations, accentuate this pluri-dimensionality, and such is the case for Med Hondo's *Lumière noire* (1992) set in Paris; Idrissa Ouedraogo's *Le cri du cœur* (1994) in Lyon; José Zeka Laplaine's *Le clandestin* (1996) in

---

8. Dina Sherzer, "Introduction," *Cinema, Colonialism, Postcolonialism,* 10.

9. Barlet, "Les nouveaux films d'Afrique sont-ils africains?" *Cinémas africains, une oasis dans le désert,* ed. Samuel Leliévre, *CinémAction* 106 (2003): 43–49. Except where noted, all translations are mine.

Portugal; and Jean-Marie Teno's *Clando* (1996) in Germany. To talk about francophone film today means ultimately going beyond the reductive parameters of a nation-centric paradigm in order to acknowledge that any discussion about France necessarily also includes Europe. Indicative of this development are measures taken by French President Nicolas Sarkozy (through the establishment in 2007 of a Ministry for Immigration, National Identity, Integration, and Co-Development) to both restrict illegal immigration and to establish co-development partnerships with "sending" countries in the *global south*. Indeed, France has attempted to extend these policies to other European Union member-states by making immigration a priority item during the French tenure of the E.U. that began on July 1, 2008.

Films such as Med Hondo's 1998 *Watani: Un monde sans mal* explored the racism, xenophobia, and right-wing politics that informed the political climate in France when on August 23, 1996 over one thousand armed CRS (Compagnies Républicaines de Sécurité) mobile police units stormed the Saint-Bernard de la Chapelle church in Paris's 18th arrondissement and forcibly removed the *sans-papiers* who had sought refuge there while awaiting a decision on their request for *régularisation* (amnesty and legalization). Yet, antecedents to these films exist. For example, as early as 1974, Inoussa Ousseini's *Paris c'est joli* highlighted the changing political climate in France toward immigrants and examples of heightened xenophobia that would culminate in Valéry Giscard d'Estaing's invocation of the need for "zero immigration" during the early years of his 1974–1981 presidency.

The compelling dimension of the *sans-papiers* question concerns the mutation, and transfer into public discourse *and* onto film, from invisibility to visibility. This has coincided with other developments; for example, the question of visibility was also prominent during the riots that took place in French cities and *banlieues* in October and November 2005 (often referred to as the "revolt of the invisibles"), although in this case the predominantly disadvantaged and disenfranchised urban populations who collectively abandoned and relinquished their economic and social invisibility in order to render observable those feelings of disaffection were mostly French citizens. In *Soleil O* (1969), Hondo criticized the racism confronting Africans in France, and also established correlations between the historical slave trade and current labor practices in the economically prosperous zones of Western Europe. Madeleine Cottenet-Hage, describing this situation, stated that "The feeling of alienation, the experience of racism that he [Hondo] encountered during these years, the exploitation of cheap, imported manual labor, and the living conditions of immigrant communities all became material for this film and the following one" ("Decolonizing," 1974)—themes to which Hondo returned in *Les bicots nègres vos voisins* (1973). But for Hondo, this corresponds to a very particular and profound political commitment: "This is the main reason why I make films. Confronted with racist representations of Africa in the media, I could only try and respond in my own way and with the means at my disposal in order to offer another version that was closer to reality."[10] According to David Murphy and Patrick Williams, "Med Hondo is acknowledged as one of the great postcolonial chroniclers of the lives of the unrecognized and unrepresented masses in the various waves of the African diaspora."[11]

The kinds of reformulations of the parameters of French cinema addressed earlier are exemplified by Hondo's claim that *Lumière noire* is to be considered "my first French film" (cited in Signaté, 111), a statement that is further complicated by the fact that we are left to fathom what he really means. After all, the film deals with previously tackled subjects such as racial discrimination and is anchored in *both* an African space (in this case Mali) *and* France. What this film does confirm, however, as Cottenet-Hage has argued, is the fact that "the existence of the French 'space' remains, at least for the time being, intricately bound to African cinema."[12] Faithfully adapted from Didier Daeninckx's 1987 novel of the same name, the action is organized around a severe blunder by the police (a "bavure policière") during which Gérard Blanc, a technician employed at Air France, is shot and killed.[13] Yves Guyot decides to investigate the suspicious death of his best friend, an undertaking complicated by conflicting "official" reports and depositions that claim to be concerned with establishing the truth: "My objective," insists judge Berthier, "is to verify all the information I am given and to synthesize the different points of view I am given" (Daeninckx, 16).

10. Ibrahima Signaté, *Med Hondo: Un cinéaste rebelle* (Paris: Présence Africaine, 1994), 75.

11. David Murphy and Patrick Williams, *Postcolonial African Cinema: Ten Directors* (Manchester: Manchester University Press, 2007), 70.

12. Cottenet-Hage, "Images of France in Francophone African Films (1978–1998)," in *Focus on African Films,* ed. Françoise Pfaff (Bloomington: Indiana University Press, 1998), 121.

13. Didier Daeninckx, *Lumière noire* (Paris: Galimard, 1987).

Two additional inquiries are also being conducted, one by the police and the other by an administrative review team; these serve to further confuse the complex process of arriving at an accurate account of events. A climate of fear and escalating xenophobia triggered by an imminent threat of a terrorist attack provides the background that partially explains the agitation and anxiety of the authorities. When they killed the innocent Gérard Blanc, they realized the negative effect this would have on public opinion: "Our task is to terrorize the terrorists, not the people we are supposed to protect!" (Daeninckx, 181). This led them to hastily elaborate a scheme that would implicate Gérard Blanc in criminal activities, "thereby justifying, after the fact, his assassination" (Daeninckx, 182), and in doing so to deploy a complex web of lies to support their version of reality.

The original incident took place in proximity to Paris's Charles de Gaulle international airport, and Guyot soon learns that there was a witness to the "crime," a Malian *sans-papiers* who was being held in detention and awaiting deportation at a nearby hotel. It turns out that the entire seventh floor of the hotel had been requisitioned for the police authorities by the Ministry of the Interior:

> It's not exactly a secret, but they're afraid that it will harm the reputation of the Artel chain if the information gets out. The Bobigny police department, or the Ministry of the Interior, well, they're the same thing I suppose, detain illegal immigrants in the rooms until they can find an aircraft to send them off. . . . They're mostly from sub-Saharan or North Africa. . . . Illegals who got caught without papers. (Daeninckx, 54)

In the established tradition of thrillers and detective stories, it turns out that the Malian witness Boudjougou (Babemba in the novel) enjoyed "a room with a view" and that his perspective from "the rear window" would be a crucial component in the process of reconstituting the events of the night in question and in solving the enigma of the crime. All the ingredients of a classic police investigation are set in motion, and Guyot's parallel investigation leads him to visit several Paris neighborhoods where he finds assistance in an expansive diasporic network. Having obtained information as to Boudjougou's whereabouts, he sets off on a voyage to Mali to follow his trail. This component of the story had served as the motivating point for Hondo, since, as he has claimed, "the spectacle in French airports of Africans chained together awaiting deportation is nauseating" (Signaté, 113). The gradual and systematic reconstruction of events, including images of the handcuffed Malians being transported to the hotel, fabricated testimony and newspaper reports, the extra-judicial elimination of witnesses, and inconsistent police reports, all serve to juxtapose a documented reality with the fabricated version of events proposed by the police authorities.

The on-screen post-script offers suggestive associations between the struggle to arrive at a truthful account of the events of the fateful night in question and racial tensions and dynamics: "This is the battle between day and night. I see black light." Drawn from Victor Hugo's well-known utterance, and partially reproducing the epigraph to Daeninckx's novel, the combat of dark and light juxtaposes the natural element with the struggle for justice addressed in the film, reconfigured around the post-Revolutionary *Déclaration des droits de l'homme et du citoyen* (as the symbolic culmination of Enlightenment). In this case, the application of the key principles of that document are questioned by Hondo when he claims that "seeing Africans chained together like criminals prior to forceful repatriation is a spectacle that does little to honor those States which claim to embrace the rights of Man and democratic ideals. Nothing is worse for a person than humiliation. This has become the daily lot of immigrants in the countries of the North" (Signaté, 72). Thus, Hondo's film ends up joining the newly-politicized discourse for visibility of the *sans-papiers* that would be enunciated a few years later as an expression of their awareness of those fundamental rights and in turn their unambiguous assertion that those rights be extended to them.

In José Zeka Laplaine's short black and white silent film *Clandestin* (15 minutes), we witness the arrival of a cargo ship loaded with multiple containers as it docks in Lisbon's harbor. A crate opens to reveal the lone figure of a young clandestine African man, abandoned on the perilous crossing by a now-deceased fellow traveler: "I traveled with an injured Angolan man. He was going to ask for political asylum . . ." As he attempts to find his way out of the docks, he is chased by a black security guard equipped with a truncheon (the irony of this individual's responsibility for patrol and surveillance is of course striking). The rapid action and movement on screen adapts some of the devices associated with animated films, a chase ensues through the streets of the Alfama, Lisbon's oldest quarter; the sound of a clock ticking away heightens the tension and suspense; the young man stops and starts, visibly petrified, tracked down like a wild animal; he gets away once, is then caught by the guard who keeps resurfacing, and then escapes again from his clutches. The act of the young African's temporarily outrunning the guard allows the camera to provide images of the lives of other Africans living on these shores, some in conditions of squalor, others driven by their precarious economic status to exploiting new arrivals. The turning point arrives when he is run over by a car. As the young African lies unconscious and, one assumes, dead in the street, the guard takes umbrage when the driver mumbles some inaudible comment, reproduced on screen in text as the term "Negro" and followed by an exclamation point. Miraculously, the fallen "adventurer" gets up again, unharmed, and the chase ensues.

An element of humor characterizes this game of cat and mouse, and one gradually senses a growing solidarity between the actors, a shared sentiment of vulnerability that comes from being perpetually scrutinized, inspected, kept under observance and surveillance. Having already seen him emerge from a container, we now learn from an on-screen inscription of the motivation for the adventure the central protagonist has begun: "My dear cousin, you must be wondering what I am up to. Well, as planned, I hid in a container and tried to join up with you in Europe. What an adventure that turned out to be." Yet, the claustrophobia of the container in which he traveled across the ocean serves to designate another metaphor of "containment," namely the plight of the clandestine undocumented subject newly arrived on the inhospitable shores of Europe. The young man is blinded by daylight upon exiting the container, and Laplaine's *Clandestin* operates a kind of intertextual gesture with Hondo's film *Lumière noire* through the invocation of the shortcomings of Enlightenment ideals as symbols of hope and emancipation, promises that have not been actualized for these displaced subjects. The choice of Portugal's capital city as the topographic space for the unfolding of the narrative is far from coincidental. Lisbon's numerous monuments, these "sites of memory" conjure up a comprehensive historical subtext that has much to reveal concerning the film's message: the history of the Alfama and the well-known symbol of the Torre de Belém. Perhaps even more importantly in this regard is the city's most famous monument, namely the Padrao dos Descobrimentos (the Monument to the Discoveries). Lisbon was, of course, the point of departure for so many navigators and explorers. These earlier "adventurers" are commemorated here for their voyages of conquest and of discovery to other shores, thereby conjuring associations between the expansionist policies of the European colonial powers and contemporary neocolonial factors that have engendered the economic unevenness between the global south and economically prosperous north and provoked the emigration of subjects across the Mediterranean.

Laplaine's film, however, warns of the dangers of such a voyage and reveals the futility of these crossings, recording instead the harsh realities of the "north." "Cousin," the young man writes, "I ended up being turned away. I don't regret anything though, except for my poor Angolan companion. For the time being, I have decided to stay in Africa and to try and make things work. Take good care of yourself, your cousin." Thus, rather than falsely glorifying the economic possibilities in Europe, Laplaine adopts the kind of standpoint that serves to demystify migration to the north, warning young people against leaving Africa. Analogous conclusions are to be found in Jean-Marie Teno's film *Clando* (1996) set partially in Germany where, as Sheila Petty shows: "Teno interrogates migration as a solution to Cameroon's problems by suggesting that it is ultimately self-defeating for the nation."[14]

In *Le cri du cœur*, Idrissa Ouedraogo turns his attention to a different facet of the African presence in France, namely the question of family reunification, a much-contested issue today as new policies have prioritized selective economic immigration. The opening sequence features Ibrahim, the father of the central protagonist Moctar, depositing a letter in a French mailbox. Only later when the letter is delivered to his wife (Saffi) in Africa, do we learn through the declarative "We are leaving for France" that after years of hard work he has now achieved a level of economic security that enables him to have his wife and son come and join him in Lyon. The originality of the scenario in this case stems from the fact that Moctar was actually born in France. Interestingly enough, this shift has stimulated critiques pertaining to "Ouédraogo's decision to move away from his West African homeland to make a film about an African family in France" (Murphy and Williams, 154). Also noteworthy is the fact that the film was a co-production of the Centre Européen Cinématographique, the Centre National de la Cinématographie de la Communauté Européenne Économique, and the Ministère Français de la Coopération and the Agence de Coopération Culturelle et Technique (ACCT), a funding structure that has set into motion partnerships that ultimately translate into a process of de-centering the sites and locations at which "African" films are made.

14. Sheila Petty, "Postcolonial Geographies: Landscape and Alienation in *Clando*," *Cinema and Social Discourse in Cameroon*, ed. Alexie Tcheuyap, *Bayreuth African Studies* 69 (2005): 170.

The *return* that takes place here is to the metropole rather than the more common reverse journey. This has the effect of forcing the viewer to rethink a number of stereotypical representations of immigrant communities, the most obvious of which concerns the perceived unwillingness of immigrants to seek integration into French society. Ibrahim's determination to reunite his family provides the motivation for enduring separation and for overcoming the obstacles he encounters to his incorporation into the French economic sphere. Paradoxically though, in this occurrence, his son experiences difficulties relinquishing his connection to the continent of Africa and to the various signifiers of that attachment. This manifests itself in the recurrent and persistent haunting visions and sightings he has of a hyena, events that prompt those around him to question his mental health. Cottenet-Hage sees in these episodes "the nightmarish translation of his anguish at separation from both his grandfather (whose totem is the hyena) and his native village" (Cottenet-Hage, "Images," 108). Moctar's difficulty with acculturation and transplantation emerges as paradigmatic of assimilationist issues concerning immigrant populations, since Moctar's difficulties at school render him visible to his teachers and to the authorities (social workers, doctors, psycho-therapists, and so on). Ibrahim states that "he's acting out to draw attention to himself" and reminds his mother that "we're foreigners here" and "you need to understand that we must be discreet. Unwanted attention could make things difficult for us." The central objective, as he sees it, is to abide by codes of Republican indistinguishability.

Ibrahim's perspective must be framed in the context of his larger struggle with employment, and his "five years of sacrifice" that allowed the family to be together again as a unit. Evoking the hardships related to work, he expresses how "times are tough," a statement that activates an intertextual reference to the wider discourse on migration when a news story is interjected into the narrative featuring the deaths of migrants on a recent attempted crossing of the Mediterranean. Paradoxically, while the family has now been brought together after years of separation marked by an ocean, the realities of their long working days in France, during which they hardly see each other as a family, introduce new forms of separation and distance whereby each family member occupies an autonomous space in "two different worlds," within the physical topography of France but also in the imaginative configuration in which Moctar finds refuge. When Moctar goes away for a few days to the countryside to clear his mind, the visit with his uncle Mamadou allows him to interact with one of his cousins who has not been to Africa. "What's it like over there?" his cousin asks. Moctar's response provides us with an indication as to some of the factors contributing to his condition, namely his feelings of isolation as a result of the long hours he spends alone while his parents strive to make ends meet, exemplified by the fact that he remembers Africa as a space in which one is never cold or alone. Responding to the imperative of achieving integration in France, Moctar's father (unlike the protagonist Paulo who befriends and listens to Moctar) is not able to equip his son with the tools he requires for transition, perhaps because he embodies the ambiguity and confusion around the notion of the "fatherland," but also because he figures as a symbol of absence for the child who has erased him from the sentiment of "togetherness" he associates with Africa.

Not surprisingly, as Thackway has shown, "the emergence of the latter themes in film is an interesting contemporary development that reflects the real fragility of immigrant status as Europe has begun to tighten its borders" (Thackway, *Africa*, 135). Filmmakers have become increasingly determined to address this precariousness and have rekindled their efforts at warning fellow Africans about the realities that await them in Europe. Images of unsuccessful Mediterranean crossings painfully stir up memories of earlier generations whose forceful displacement cannot be occluded. Connecting and insisting upon the longer history of African/French/European relations effectively brings to the surface the shortcomings inherent to monolithic interpretations of history that fail to adequately account for the constitutive aspects of the African/French experience, one that extends to cross-cultural influences in film and literature.

# Contributors

GUY AUSTIN is Reader in French at the University of Sheffield, UK and the author of *Contemporary French Cinema* (MUP, 1996), *Claude Chabrol* (MUP, 1999) and *Stars in Modern French Film* (Arnold, 1999), as well as of various articles and chapters on modern French cinema. He is currently researching filmic representations of the Algerian War, and has just had an article on Algerian cinema and the war published in *French Studies* (February 2007).

JAMES F. AUSTIN is Assistant Professor of French and Film at Connecticut College (New London, CT). He took his Ph.D. from Yale University in 2003. Austin has written on the construction of French identity in the digital French heritage films of 2001 ("Digitizing Frenchness in 2001: On a 'Historic' Moment in the French Cinema," *French Cultural Studies*), and on Marcel Proust, pastiche, and French education ("Pastiche Expelled: A Proustian Guide to French Pedagogy," *Dalhousie French Studies*). His book, *Proust, Pastiche, and the Postmodern, or, Why Style Matters* is forthcoming from Bucknell University Press.

ROGER CELESTIN is Professor of French and comparative literary and cultural studies at the University of Connecticut. He is the author of *From Cannibals to Radicals, Figures and Limits of Exoticism*; co-author of *Universalism in Crisis: France From 1851 to The Present*, and co-editor of *Beyond French Feminisms: Debates on Women, Politics, and Culture in France, 1981–2001*. He is founding editor and co-editor of *Contemporary French & Francophone Studies: SITES*.

LUDOVIC CORTADE, an alum of the École Normale Supérieure, is Assistant Professor in the French Department of New York University,

**YFS 115,** *New Spaces for French and Francophone Cinema*, ed. James F. Austin, © 2009 by Yale University.

where he teaches French cinema theory and aesthetics. His current research is on representation of landscape in French cinema as well as the influence of the French geographical school on the writings of André Bazin. He recently co-edited, with Margaret Flinn, a special issue of *Contemporary French Civilization* on the New Wave. His book, *Le cinéma de l'immobilité* (Paris: Publications de la Sorbonne, 2008), has just been published.

MARGARET C. FLINN is Assistant Professor of French and Cinema Studies at the University of Illinois at Urbana-Champaign. She has published on subjects such as the film theory of Elie Faure, and women in North African cinema, and has co-edited two special issues on the cinema: "Ce que le cinéma fait à la littérature (et réciproquement)," *Fabula: Littérature Histoire, Théorie,* with Jean-Louis Jeannelle, and "The New Wave at 50," *Contemporary French Civilization,* with Ludovic Cortade. Currently, she is a completing a book entitled *Bodies in Space: The Social Architecture of French Cinema, 1929–39.*

MICHEL MARIE is Professor of Cinema at the Université de Paris 3: Sorbonne Nouvelle, where he has taught since 1972. Since 1988, he has directed the "Cinéma et image" imprint at the Nathan and Armand Colin publishing houses. He has co-written, with Jacques Aumont, several of the most commonly used texts in teaching cinema, *Esthétique du film* (Nathan, 1983), *L'analyse des films* (Nathan, 1988), and *Le dictionnaire théorique et critique du cinéma* (Nathan, 2000, 2008). His recent books include: *Le cinéma muet,* Cahiers du cinéma, 2005; *Comprendre Godard, travelling avant sur* A bout de souffle *et* Le mépris (Armand Colin, 2006); *Le guide des études cinématographiques et audiovisuelles* (Armand Colin, 2006); *Lire les images de cinéma* (with Laurent Jullier) (Larousse, 2007). Marie has also edited or contributed to numerous anthologies on the French cinema.

PANIVONG NORINDR is chair of the Department of French and Italian at the University of Southern California. His most recent essays on cinema include "Enlisting Early Cinema in the Service of 'la plus grande France,'" in Richard Abel, Giorgio Bertellini, Rob King, eds., *Early Cinema and the 'National'* (John Libbey Publishing, 2008) and "Angkor filmée: de l'exotisme à l'identité nationale," in Hughes Tertrais, ed. *Angkor VIIIe–XXIe siècle: Mémoire et identité khmères* (Autrement, 2008). He is currently completing a book entitled *(Post)Colonial Screens.*

CATHERINE PORTUGES is Professor and Graduate Program Director in the Department of Comparative Literature at the University of Massachusetts, Amherst, where she also is director of the film studies program. She has published many essays on the cinema, and is the author of *Screen Memories: The Hungarian Cinema of Márta Mészáros*, and has co-edited books on gender and central European cinema (*Gendered Subjects: the Dynamics of Feminist Pedagogy*, 1985; *Cinema in Transition: Post-socialist East Central Europe*, forthcoming).

SALLY SHAFTO is an independent film scholar who has spent most of the past decade living in Paris. In 2007 her study of the Zanzibar films was published in a bilingual edition by the Éditions Paris Expérimental. She is currently collaborating on an exhibition of psychedelic art in France at the CAPC Musée d'Art Contemporain in Bordeaux.

DOMINIC THOMAS is chair of the Departments of French and Francophone Studies and Italian and Professor of Comparative Literature at the University of California Los Angeles. He is the author of *Nation-Building, Propaganda and Literature in Francophone Africa* (Indiana University Press, 2002) and *Black France: Colonialism, Immigration and Transnationalism* (Indiana University Press, 2007).

The following issues are available through **Yale University Press,** Customer Service Department, P.O. Box 209040, New Haven, CT 06520-9040. Tel. 1-800-405-1619. yalebooks.com

69 The Lesson of Paul de Man (1985) $22.00

73 Everyday Life (1987) $22.00

75 The Politics of Tradition: Placing Women in French Literature (1988) $22.00

Special Issue: After the Age of Suspicion: The French Novel Today (1989) $22.00

76 Autour de Racine: Studies in Intertextuality (1989) $22.00

77 Reading the Archive: On Texts and Institutions (1990) $22.00

78 On Bataille (1990) $22.00

79 Literature and the Ethical Question (1991) $22.00

Special Issue: Contexts: Style and Value in Medieval Art and Literature (1991) $22.00

80 Baroque Topographies: Literature/History/ Philosophy (1992) $22.00

81 On Leiris (1992) $22.00

82 Post/Colonial Conditions Vol. 1 (1993) $22.00

83 Post/Colonial Conditions Vol. 2 (1993) $22.00

84 Boundaries: Writing and Drawing (1993) $22.00

85 Discourses of Jewish Identity in 20th-Century France (1994) $22.00

86 Corps Mystique, Corps Sacré (1994) $22.00

87 Another Look, Another Woman (1995) $22.00

88 Depositions: Althusser, Balibar, Macherey (1995) $22.00

89 Drafts (1996) $22.00

90 Same Sex / Different Text? Gay and Lesbian Writing in French (1996) $22.00

91 Genet: In the Language of the Enemy (1997) $22.00

92 Exploring the Conversible World (1997) $22.00

93 The Place of Maurice Blanchot (1998) $22.00

94 Libertinage and Modernity (1999) $22.00

95 Rereading Allegory: Essays in Memory of Daniel Poirion (1999) $22.00

96 50 Years of *Yale French Studies,* Part I: 1948-1979 (1999) $22.00

97 50 Years of *Yale French Studies,* Part 2: 1980-1998 (2000) $22.00

98 The French Fifties (2000) $22.00

99 Jean-François Lyotard: Time and Judgment (2001) $22.00

100 FRANCE/USA: The Cultural Wars (2001) $22.00

101 Fragments of Revolution (2002) $22.00

102 Belgian Memories (2002) $22.00

103 French and Francophone: the Challenge of Expanding Horizons (2003) $22.00

104 Encounters with Levinas (2003) $22.00

105 Pereckonings: Reading Georges Perec (2004) $22.00

106 Jean Paulhan's Fiction, Criticism, and Editorial Activity (2004) $22.00

107 The Haiti Issue (2005) $22.00

108 Crime Fictions (2005) $22.00

109 Surrealism and Its Others (2006) $22.00

110 Meaning and Its Objects (2006) $22.00

111 Myth and Modernity (2007) $22.00

112 The Transparency of the Text (2007) $22.00

113 French Education: Fifty Years Later (2008) $22.00

114 Writing and the Image Today (2008) $22.00

---

**ORDER FORM** **Yale University Press,** P.O. Box 209040, New Haven, CT 06520-9040

I would like to purchase the following individual issues:

_____

For individual issues, please add postage and handling:

Single issue, United States $2.75          Each additional issue $.50

Single issue, foreign countries $5.00          Each additional issue $1.00

Connecticut residents please add sales tax of 6%.

Payment of $_____ is enclosed (including sales tax if applicable).

MasterCard no. _____ Expiration date _____

VISA no. _____ Expiration date _____

Signature _____

SHIP TO _____

_____

---

See the next page for ordering other back issues. Yale French Studies is also available through Xerox University Microfilms, 300 North Zeeb Road, Ann Arbor, MI 48106.

The following issues are still available through the **Yale French Studies Office,** P.O. Box 208251, New Haven, CT 06520-8251.

| | | |
|---|---|---|
| 19/20 Contemporary Art $3.50 | 42 Zola $5.00 | 54 Mallarmé $5.00 |
| 33 Shakespeare $3.50 | 43 The Child's Part $5.00 | 61 Toward a Theory of Description $6.00 |
| 35 Sade $3.50 | 45 Language as Action $5.00 | |
| 39 Literature and Revolution $3.50 | 46 From Stage to Street $3.50 | |
| | 52 Graphesis $5.00 | |

### Add for postage & handling

| | |
|---|---|
| Single issue, United States $3.85 (Priority Mail) | Each additional issue $1.25 |
| Single issue, United States $1.90 (Third Class) | Each additional issue $ .50 |
| Single issue, foreign countries $3.75 (Book Rate) | Each additional issue $3.00 |

**YALE FRENCH STUDIES,** P.O. Box 208251, New Haven, Connecticut 06520-8251
A check made payable to YFS is enclosed. Please send me the following issue(s):

Issue no.                          Title                                                           Price

_____

_____

Postage & handling _____

Total _____

Name _____

Number/Street _____

City _____ State _____ Zip _____

- - - - - - - - - - - - - - - - - - - - - - - - - - - - - - - - - - - - - - - - - - - - - - - - - - - - -

The following issues are now available through Periodicals Service Company, 11 Main Street, Germantown, N.Y. 12526, Phone: (518) 537-4700. Fax: (518) 537-5899.

| | |
|---|---|
| 1 Critical Bibliography of Existentialism | 19/20 Contemporary Art |
| 2 Modern Poets | 21 Poetry Since the Liberation |
| 3 Criticism & Creation | 22 French Education |
| 4 Literature & Ideas | 23 Humor |
| 5 The Modern Theatre | 24 Midnight Novelists |
| 6 France and World Literature | 25 Albert Camus |
| 7 André Gide | 26 The Myth of Napoleon |
| 8 What's Novel in the Novel | 27 Women Writers |
| 9 Symbolism | 28 Rousseau |
| 10 French-American Literature Relationships | 29 The New Dramatists |
| 11 Eros, Variations... | 30 Sartre |
| 12 God & the Writer | 31 Surrealism |
| 13 Romanticism Revisited | 32 Paris in Literature |
| 14 Motley: Today's French Theater | 33 Shakespeare in France |
| 15 Social & Political France | 34 Proust |
| 16 Foray through Existentialism | 48 French Freud |
| 17 The Art of the Cinema | 51 Approaches to Medieval Romance |
| 18 Passion & the Intellect, or Malraux | |

36/37 Structuralism has been reprinted by Doubleday as an Anchor Book.
55/56 Literature and Psychoanalysis has been reprinted by Johns Hopkins University Press, and can be ordered through Customer Service, Johns Hopkins University Press, Baltimore, MD 21218.